TOP-RATED
FLOWERING
TREES
AND HOW TO USE THEM IN YOUR GARDEN

This book was produced for Western Publishing Company, Inc., by the staff of Horticultural Associates, Inc., in cooperation with Amfac Garden Products.

Executive Producer: Richard Ray
Contributing Authors: John Ford, Robert L. Ticknor
Consultants: Claire Barrett, Fred Galle, Ralph Miller, Carl A. Totemeier, Richard Turner, Joseph A. Witt
Photography: Michael Landis
Art Director: Richard Baker
Book Design: Judith Hemmerich
Associate Editors: Michael MacCaskey, Lance Walheim
Research Editor: Randy Peterson
Copy Editors: Greg Boucher, Miriam Boucher
Production Editor: Kathleen Parker
Book Production: Lingke Moeis
Illustrations: Charles Hoeppner, Roy Jones
Typography: Linda Encinas
Additional Photography: William Aplin, Susan A. Roth
Cover Photo: Michael Landis
Acknowledgements: Jim Gibbons, Horticulturist, San Diego Wild Animal Park, Escondido, CA; Chuck Kline, Horticulturist, Sea World, San Diego, CA; Bill Knerr and Robert Ward, Horticulturists, Zoological Society of San Diego, San Diego, CA; Henry Koide, Presidio Garden Center, San Diego, CA; Bill Robinson, Japanese Garden Society of Oregon.

For Western Publishing Company, Inc.:
Editorial Director: Jonathan P. Latimer
Senior Editor: Susan A. Roth
Copy Editor: Karen Stray Nolting

3 **Top-Rated Flowering Trees**
4 Climates for Flowering Trees
5 Regional Adaptation Charts

9 **Using Flowering Trees in Your Garden**
16 Landscape Use Lists

21 **A Guide to Top-Rated Flowering Trees**

53 **Caring for Flowering Trees**
60 Planting and Care Charts
63 Name Cross-Reference
64 Index

Golden Press • **New York**

Western Publishing Company, Inc.

Racine, Wisconsin

Top-Rated Flowering Trees

This book is designed to help you select the most appropriate flowering trees to meet the landscape needs around your home. It also provides planting and care information to help assure success in growing the trees you plant.

The trees described in this book are widely used, readily available, and dependable. Growers, gardeners, and horticulturists judged them top-rated, based on first-hand experience. The top-rated flowering trees for your region are shown in the charts on pages 5 to 7.

Shrub or tree: It is sometimes difficult to categorize a plant as either a shrub or a tree. Trees are usually thought of as tall plants with high branches and single trunks, and shrubs as plants with low branches, a full shape, and many stems. However, pruning and training can change a shrub into a tree and vice versa. If a shrub can be used as a tree, it may be included in this book.

Living color: When in bloom, flowering trees make a bold visual statement. Though you grow them primarily to enjoy the blossoms, flowering trees are part of your garden year-round. Depending on the particular plant you select, you might also use a flowering tree to shade a patio, block an unsightly view, or soften the lines of your house.

Names: The common names of plants vary from region to region, so the botanical names, which are universally accepted, are used in this book. The chart on page 63 matches the most widely used common names with the proper botanical names.

At left: Dogwoods *(Cornus sp.)* bloom in early spring. Colorful fruits follow in summer preceding brilliant fall leaf color.

Crab apple *(Malus sp.)*

Flowering plum *(Prunus sp.)*

Kaffirboom coral tree *(Erythrina sp.)*

Jacaranda *(Jacaranda sp.)*

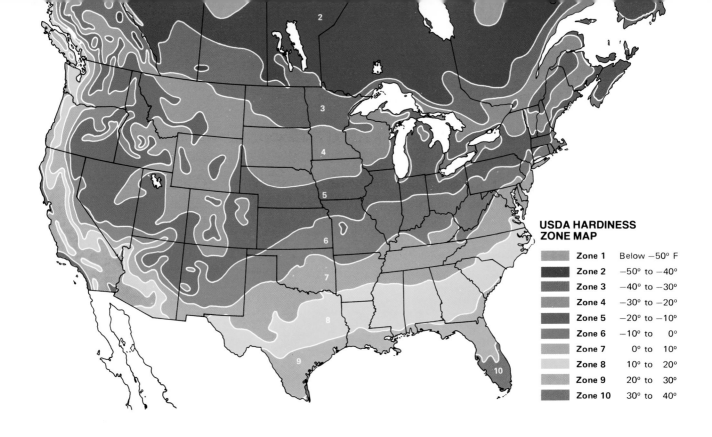

USDA HARDINESS ZONE MAP

	Zone 1	Below −50° F
	Zone 2	−50° to −40°
	Zone 3	−40° to −30°
	Zone 4	−30° to −20°
	Zone 5	−20° to −10°
	Zone 6	−10° to 0°
	Zone 7	0° to 10°
	Zone 8	10° to 20°
	Zone 9	20° to 30°
	Zone 10	30° to 40°

Climates for Flowering Trees

The plant hardiness map shows the average low temperatures throughout the United States and Southern Canada. It divides North America into 10 zones with the average minimum temperature of each zone differing by 10 degrees fahrenheit. All plants in this book are identified in the following charts and in the encyclopedia by the zones where they are considered to be top-rated. Use the map to find your hardiness zone so you can select appropriate plants for your garden.

As every gardener learns, cold hardiness is only one factor of a plant's adaptation. A plant's ability to do well in a certain location depends on unique combinations of soil type, wind, rainfall, length and time of cold, humidity, summer temperatures, and temperatures in relation to humidity. For example, the large-leaved catalpa would be a poor choice to plant unprotected in the windy areas of the desert because its leaves are susceptible to wind damage. But given wind protection by larger trees or buildings it could prosper there.

Many plants require a certain amount of winter cold to flower and begin spring growth. Oriental flowering cherry trees bloom well in Washington D.C., the Northwest, and Northern California, but do not blossom as prolifically in Southern California or along the Gulf Coast where the winters are too warm to provide a sufficient cold period.

The USDA hardiness zone map does not take other climate factors into consideration. To give you additional information the map and charts on the following pages break down the United States into 10 climate regions. For a plant to be adapted to your area, it should be recommended for your USDA hardiness zone and your climate region. For example, *Acacia baileyana* is recommended for USDA hardiness Zone 9, a zone including portions of both western and southern United States. Climates in these two portions of Zone 9 are remarkably different. *Acacia baileyana* does well only in warm, dry areas of the West. USDA Zones 8 to 10 are particularly

complex in the western United States. Many plants with a southern range of Zone 8 can also be grown in Zones 9 and 10 in the West. In these cases, it is best to follow regional recommendations.

The climates around your home:
Another important aspect of climate is microclimate, the small climates around your home that differ slightly from the general climate of your area. The northern side of your property, which is probably partially shaded most of the day by your house, is a cool microclimate. The southern side of your home, which, unless shaded by trees, receives hot sun almost all day, is a warm microclimate. A good way to become aware of microclimates is by making a site plan. (See page 10.)

Plants that are borderline for your area may do well if you take protective measures such as providing wind or snow shelters and selecting a planting location that takes advantage of your property's microclimates.

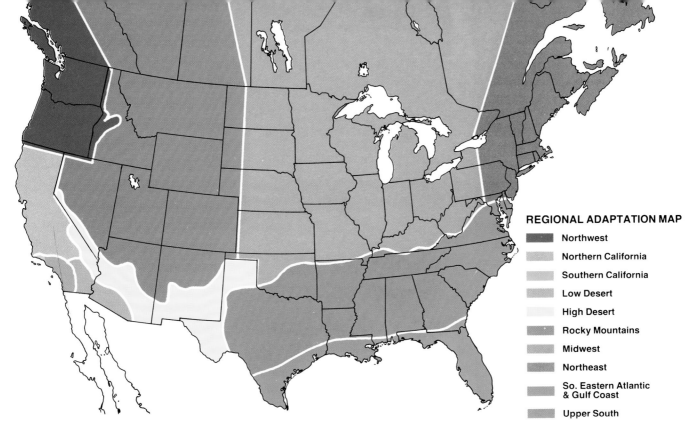

REGIONAL ADAPTATION MAP
- Northwest
- Northern California
- Southern California
- Low Desert
- High Desert
- Rocky Mountains
- Midwest
- Northeast
- So. Eastern Atlantic & Gulf Coast
- Upper South

Regional Adaptation

PLANT NAME	ZONES	NORTHWEST	NORTHERN CALIFORNIA	SOUTHERN CALIFORNIA	LOW DESERT	HIGH DESERT	ROCKY MOUNTAINS	MIDWEST	NORTHEAST	SO. EASTERN ATLANTIC & GULF COAST	UPPER SOUTH
Acacia baileyana	9		■	■	■						
Aesculus x carnea	5-9	■	■				■	■	■		■
Aesculus hippocastanum	4-8	■	■				■	■	■		■
Albizia julibrissin	7-10	■	■	■	■	■			■	■	■
Amelanchier sp.	4-8	■	■				■	■	■		■
Bauhinia variegata	9-10		■	■						■	
Callistemon sp.	8-10		■	■	■					■	■
Cassia excelsa	10		■								
Catalpa sp.	5-10	■	■	■	■	■	■	■	■	■	■
Cercis canadensis	4-7	■	■				■*	■	■	■	■
Cercis occidentalis	7-10	■	■	■	■	■					
Chionanthus virginicus	5-9	■						■	■	■	■
Citrus sp.	9-10		■	■	■					■	
Cornus florida	5-9	■	■	■				■	■	■	■
Cornus kousa	6-9	■	■	■				■	■	■	■
Crataegus sp.	5-9	■	■			■	■*	■	■		■
Erythrina caffra	9-10			■						■	
Erythrina coralloides	9-10			■	■					■	
Erythrina crista-galli	9-10		■	■	■					■	
Erythrina humeana	9-10			■	■					■	

*Low elevation areas

Crab apples *(Malus sp.)* grow in almost all areas of the country.

Regional Adaptation

PLANT NAME	ZONES	NORTHWEST	NORTHERN CALIFORNIA	SOUTHERN CALIFORNIA	LOW DESERT	HIGH DESERT	ROCKY MOUNTAINS	MIDWEST	NORTHEAST	SO. EASTERN ATLANTIC & GULF COAST	UPPER SOUTH
Eucalyptus sp.	7-10		■	■	■	■				■	
Franklinia alatamaha	6-8	■						■	■		■
Halesia sp.	5-8	■	■					■	■		■
Jacaranda mimosifolia	9-10		■	■						■	
Koelreuteria bipinnata	5-9		■	■	■	■	■*	■	■	■	■
Koelreuteria paniculata	5-9	■	■	■	■	■	■*	■	■	■	■
Laburnum x watereri 'Vossii'	6-9	■	■	■				■	■		■
Lagerstroemia indica	7-9	■	■	■	■	■			■	■	■
Liriodendron tulipifera	5-9	■	■	■			■	■	■	■	■
Magnolia grandiflora	7-10	■	■	■		■			■	■	■
Magnolia x soulangiana	5-10	■	■	■				■	■	■	■
Magnolia stellata	5-10	■	■					■	■	■	■
Malus floribunda	4-8	■	■	■		■	■	■	■		■
Malus 'Radiant'	4-8	■	■	■		■	■	■	■		■
Malus 'Red Jade'	4-8	■	■	■		■	■	■	■		■
Malus 'Snowdrift'	4-8	■	■	■		■	■	■	■		■
Malus x zumi 'Calocarpa'	4-8	■	■	■		■	■	■	■		■
Melaleuca linariifolia	9-10		■	■						■	
Melaleuca quinquenervia	9-10		■	■						■	

*Low elevation areas

This unusual small flowering specimen tree is a carefully trained vining wisteria *(Wisteria sp.)*.

Regional Adaptation

PLANT NAME	ZONES	NORTHWEST	NORTHERN CALIFORNIA	SOUTHERN CALIFORNIA	LOW DESERT	HIGH DESERT	ROCKY MOUNTAINS	MIDWEST	NORTHEAST	SO. EASTERN ATLANTIC & GULF COAST	UPPER SOUTH
Nerium oleander	8-10		■	■	■	■				■	■
Oxydendrum arboreum	6-9	■	■					■	■	■	■
Parkinsonia aculeata	8-10		■	■	■					■	■
Prunus x blireiana	5-9	■	■	■	■	■	■*	■	■		■
Prunus caroliniana	7-10		■	■	■	■	■*			■	■
Prunus cerasifera 'Atropurpurea'	5-9	■	■	■			■*	■	■		■
Prunus x cistena	3-9	■	■	■		■	■	■	■		■
Prunus serrulata	6-9	■	■						■		■
Prunus subhirtella	6-9	■	■						■		■
Pyrus calleryana 'Bradford'	5-9	■	■	■		■	■*	■	■	■	■
Pyrus kawakamii	9-10		■	■	■						
Robinia x ambigua 'Idahoensis'	5-10	■	■	■	■	■	■	■	■		■
Robinia pseudoacacia	3-9	■	■	■	■	■	■	■	■	■	■
Sophora japonica	5-8	■	■	■		■	■*	■	■		■
Sorbus aucuparia	2-7	■	■				■	■	■		■
Stewartia pseudocamellia	6-9	■	■						■		■
Styrax japonicus	6-9	■	■	■		■		■	■		■
Wisteria floribunda	5-9	■	■	■	■	■	■	■	■	■	■
Wisteria sinensis	5-9	■	■	■	■	■	■	■	■	■	■

*Low elevation areas

Using Flowering Trees in Your Garden

Tree selection is best approached as if you were choosing a multipurpose tool. The right tree is the one that can perform all the jobs you need it to do. The first step in choosing a flowering tree is deciding where to plant it and what function, besides providing a floral display, you want it to perform.

A complete lesson in landscaping is beyond the scope of this book, however, the following examples of how you can use flowering trees demonstrate their versatility.

LANDSCAPE USES

Accent: An accent tree is one that, because of its shape, size, and pretty flowers, will become a focal point but won't overpower the whole garden. It complements the plants around it.

Specimen: Because of its dramatic appearance both in and out of bloom, a specimen tree is used alone in a spot where it will command attention without other plants competing with it.

Shade tree: Tall trees with a thick foliage cover can provide welcome shade. Grass and many garden plants will not grow well beneath trees that cast heavy shade.

Street tree: Trees used to line streets must be durable plants that can tolerate exhaust, possible road salt, compacted soil, and other abuses. Tree shape should not interfere with traffic or pedestrians.

Lawn tree: A flowering tree that casts only light shade and has deep roots allows grass to grow beneath its boughs, making it suitable for planting in an expanse of lawn.

At Left: Flowering cherry *(Prunus sp.)* blooms in spring. They cast light shade and are good trees to garden under.

Grapefruit *(Citrus sp.)*

Crape myrtle *(Lagerstroemia indica)*

Bailey acacia *(Acacia baileyana)*

Flowering cherry *(Prunus sp.)*

Saucer magnolia trees *(Magnolia x soulangiana)* provide bright color and soften the lines of the house.

Oleander trees *(Nerium oleander)* can be used as a colorful hedge for blocking views or noise.

A purple orchid tree *(Bauhinia variegata)* forms a graceful silhouette, softening a stark white wall.

Soften architectural lines: Small trees planted near a house will blend the building into the garden setting.

Transition: Low-growing flowering trees, such as the star magnolia, can form a colorful visual transition between a garden bed and taller shade trees.

Privacy screen: Some flowering trees, such as oleander, can serve as colorful hedgelike trees that block unwanted views and viewers.

Stopgap-filler: A quick grower used to cover a space in the garden created by an unexpected plant loss. Eucalyptus and catalpa are well suited to this task.

Late color: Flowering trees are usually thought of as blooming in the spring, but some of them bloom riotously throughout the entire summer. Bottlebrush, crape myrtle, and silk tree flower profusely during the hot months. Coordinated with other flowering plants, they can help give a continuous spectrum of color in your garden. Also, trees with colorful berries or fruits provide off-season decoration.

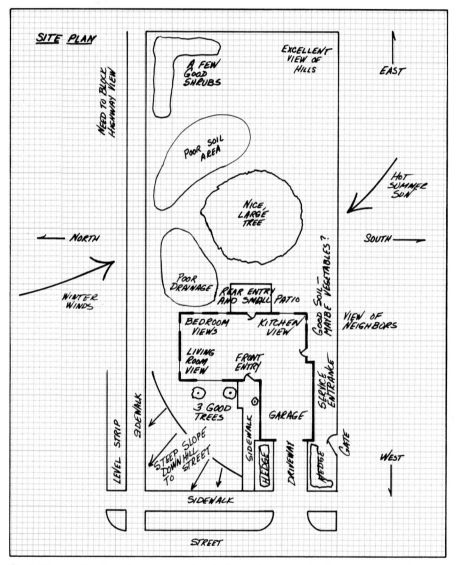

Sketching a site plan of your property, similar to the example shown above, helps you identify the landscape needs of your property. Once you note which views need to be blocked or preserved, where shade is needed, areas of poor soil or bad drainage, and paths of movement, you can begin to choose plants that meet your specific landscape requirements.

Entryways are special landscape situations. Choose plants that are attractive during a long period of time or combine plants that have outstanding features in different seasons. Here, flowering trees have been used to shade the front door, frame the walk, and provide an interesting pattern on a plain wall.

Container plants: Many flowering trees thrive in tight quarters, and make it possible to enjoy their blooms up close in large planters on decks, porches, and patios.

SITE PLAN

If you intend extensive planting or garden remodeling, a site plan is very helpful. A site plan is a sketch or diagram, drawn to scale, of your house and yard. It shows the location of doors, windows, and rooms, and existing plants, decks, or patios—anything that affects your planting. It also notes other physical aspects of your property, such as good and bad views from both indoors and out, prevailing winds, low spots and slopes, paths of air circulation, and sun patterns.

Done properly, a site plan takes a good deal of time and observation to prepare. You will need to note which areas are sunny in summer, shady in winter, and vice versa, as well as understand how winds change from season to season. These observations will help you choose the right flowering tree for a particular spot. Even if you need only one tree, close observation of the planting site is necessary. Ask yourself questions such as: Is this a cool, shady spot most of the year? Is there intense heat and light reflected from a nearby wall? Is there strong wind?

Then ask yourself questions such as: Which tree is right for a small patio? Which tree can be sheared into a hedge? Which will provide pink flowers in spring and dense shade in summer? Should I plant something that will bear edible fruit? Which tree is best to use along the west side of my house to block hot sun and save on air conditioning costs? Which tree will shut out the view of the neighbors and when will it be big enough to do so?

Once you have determined what roles the tree must play, consider the physical characteristics you can choose from.

PLANT CHARACTERISTICS

Evergreen or Deciduous: Evergreen trees block sun and wind year-round. Deciduous ones do so only during the growing season. In cold climates deciduous trees let in warm winter sun, but strategically placed evergreens will stop cold winter winds.

Habit: Consider how tall and wide a tree will be at maturity and how it will affect the surrounding landscape once it is full-grown. Few small homes can comfortably accommodate a really large tree such as a horse chestnut. In choosing a tree, it's often a good idea to examine a mature specimen in your neighborhood or local park.

Algerian tangerines *(Citrus sp.)* are excellent container trees for patio or porch use.

Redbuds *(Cercis sp.)* provide summer shade and let in winter sun.

Bradford Callery pear *(Pyrus calleryana)* has white blooms in spring. Dark green foliage turns brilliant colors in fall.

Although all trees have individual growth characteristics, it is possible to encourage or modify natural tendencies according to what your garden demands. You will, however, save a good deal of work by choosing a tree whose natural tendencies fit the site.

Though you are choosing a tree primarily for its blossoms, you must also consider how it looks when it's not in bloom. The size and shape of leaves, and whether they are fine- or bold-textured, determines how a tree blends in with other plants, and the texture influences how large, or small, an area appears to be. Small, delicate leaves can make a small patio seem larger. Heavy-textured, bold leaves can make a large area seem smaller.

Rate of Growth: If you want an immediate effect, choose a fast-growing flowering tree. But beware. Many of the fastest growing trees have undesirable characteristics, such as weak wood, excessive litter, or invasive roots.

If quick results are a must, such as in an unbearably hot area crying for shade or in a windy site desperately needing protection, consider interplanting fast-growing trees with

slower species. As the slower-growing trees reach functional size, remove the less desirable species.

Maintenance: Certain trees require less pruning, watering, spraying, or cleanup than others. (See pages 60 to 62 to determine how much care a given tree requires.)

Blossoms: Bloom season and flower color are obviously important. Most flowering trees bloom in spring, but there are also summer-flowering trees and trees that scatter bloom throughout the year.

Many flowering trees come in more than one color. Flower colors can have strikingly different effects on the landscape. White is a natural choice to lighten up shaded areas or to cool hot spots. White dogwoods flowering beneath an evergreen forest cover, a familar sight in many parts of the country, is a perfect example of how white can lighten up shaded areas. Blue is also a cool, soothing color. Yellows and reds are generally vibrant, warm colors that can make a cool spot seem warm— or a hot area even hotter.

Choose flower colors with a painter's eye. Be sure a flowering tree blends with or complements nearby plants that are in bloom at the same time. Keep the color of your house

The size and shape of a yard can be visually transformed by careful landscape planning. One solution to the problem of a small narrow lot is to give the illusion of space by creating movement toward the side property lines with a meandering pathway, and by screening the farthest boundary.

Plant form and texture, primarily determined by leaf size and shape, and flower color, can influence the apparent size of an area. Coarse textures, bold forms, hot colors, as shown above left, can make a garden seem smaller. Fine textures, delicate or simple forms, and cool colors, as illustrated above right, can make the same space seem larger. By selecting appropriate plants you can create an illusion of open space or warm intimacy in your garden.

Deciduous flowering trees are effective energy savers. In summer their shade blocks hot sun, keeping your house cool and reducing cooling costs. In winter their bare branches let sunlight through, warming your house and reducing heating costs.

Japanese dogwood *(Cornus kousa)* blooms late in spring, bears colorful fruits, and has spectacular autumn foliage.

Catalpa 'Nana' *(Catalpa bignonioides)* is a dwarf variety useful in small areas.

Flowering dogwoods *(Cornus florida)* grow best in the shade of taller trees.

in mind when choosing flower colors. For instance, setting a white flowering dogwood beside a white house would lessen the impact of the flowers, while the same tree would be nicely highlighted against a green, brown, or blue house.

Special features: Once you decide what kind of tree you need, look for additional ornamental features. Fall foliage color, brightly colored fruit, or an attractive winter silhouette can make a tree a beautiful year-round addition to the garden.

Edible fruit: Flowering trees offer more than the beauty of flowers and practical landscape applications. Some produce fruit that is good to eat. Consider including "ornamental edibles" in your planting. Citrus is an outstanding example. Leaves are glossy, dark green, clean and fresh; flowers snowy-white and wonderfully fragrant; and the fruit delicious. In colder climates many gardeners grow citrus in containers outdoors, moving them indoors for the winter.

Flowering plums produce small, tart fruits that are excellent eaten fresh, canned, or used for jelly. Pickled crab apples are a connoisseur's delight, and serviceberry fruit is savored by those who know about it.

THE OUTDOOR ROOM

Visualizing your backyard or entryway as an outdoor room is often helpful in creating a comfortable outdoor living area. Think in three dimensions and use the same requirements you would for an indoor room. A patio, porch, deck, or lawn can be your floor. Hedges, shrubs, or fences serve as walls to provide enclosure, privacy, and a sense of security. A large tree or arbor blocks strong sunlight and is the roof. Specimen and accent plants fill blank corners. Paths allow easy access from one area to another. Barbecues and sink areas are included for the outdoor cook and there is a play area for the children. This approach may not be applicable in every yard but re-creating what you like inside on the outside can make an outdoor area as livable as any indoor room.

SELECTION AID

The lists that follow will help you choose the right tree. They describe trees that solve problems, have specific attractions, or fit into difficult climate conditions.

Use these lists as an introduction to the descriptions of flowering trees in the plant encyclopedia section, pages 22 to 51. Do not decide on any tree until you have read its description. If a tree is listed in a chart without a specific species, such as *Cornus sp.*, it means there are several species to choose from. You must go to the individual plant description for information needed to make a valid choice.

Unwanted views may be hidden by closely planted evergreens, which also direct the eye to pleasant views. This green backdrop also highlights spring-flowering trees. A large deciduous flowering tree, positioned to shade the patio and house part of the day, also serves as a ceiling.

Judicious use of several small flowering trees provides shade for the front door and creates a welcome feeling. Trees are chosen to provide an extended season of color. Evergreen hedging is used to screen and define the parking area. Broad steps give easy access to the front door.

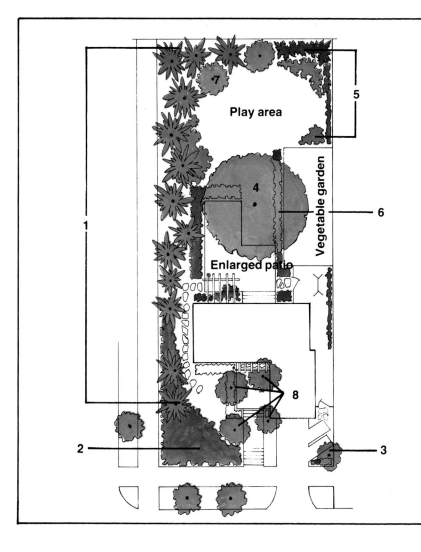

Final Landscape Plan

This example of a complete landscape plan is one way the problems identified by the site plan on page 10 might be solved.

1. Dense planting of evergreen trees blocks the unwanted view, buffers highway noise, and provides privacy.

2. Ground cover planting provides erosion control on steep slope.

3. Hedges and small trees screen and define parking area.

4. A large deciduous flowering tree shades patio and house creating a comfortable outdoor living area.

5. Low planting of evergreens frames attractive view.

6. Low hedge hides vegetable garden.

7. Spring-flowering accent tree is backdropped by contrasting evergreen foliage.

8. Small flowering trees that bloom in different seasons, provide shade and make a visually pleasing front entrance.

Dogwood (*Cornus florida*)

English hawthorn (*Crataegus laevigata*)

Golden-chain tree (*Laburnum sp.*)

Flowering Tree Landscape Use Lists

Color in More Than One Season

With any combination of flowers, fruit, fall color, or interesting bark, these trees are highlights in the landscape for many months of the year.

		Zones
Amelanchier sp.	Serviceberry	4-8
Cercis sp.	Redbud	4-10
Citrus sp.	Citrus	9-10
Cornus sp.	Dogwood	5-9
Crataegus sp.	Hawthorn	5-9
Koelreuteria sp.		
	Golden-Rain Tree	5-9
Lagerstroemia indica		
	Crape Myrtle	7-9
Malus sp.	Crab Apple	4-8
Oxydendrum arboreum		
	Sourwood	6-9
Prunus sp.	Flowering Fruit	3-10
Pyrus calleryana	Callery Pear	5-9
Sophora japonica		
	Japanese Pagoda Tree	5-8
Sorbus aucuparia		
	European Mountain Ash	2-7
Stewartia pseudocamellia		
	Japanese Stewartia	6-9
Styrax japonicus		
	Japanese Snowbell	6-9

White Blossoms

		Zones
Aesculus hippocastanum 'Alba'		
	White Horse Chestnut	4-8
Amelanchier sp.	Serviceberry	4-8
Catalpa sp.	Catalpa	5-10
Chionanthus virginicus		
	Fringe Tree	5-9
Citrus sp.	Citrus	9-10
Cornus sp.	Dogwood	5-9
Crataegus sp.	Hawthorn	5-9
Eucalyptus sp.	Eucalyptus	7-10
Franklinia alatamaha		
	Franklin Tree	6-8
Halesia sp.	Silver-Bell	5-8
Lagerstroemia indica		
	Crape Myrtle	7-9
Magnolia sp.	Magnolia	5-10
Malus floribunda		
	Japanese Flowering Crab Apple	4-8
Malus 'Red Jade'		
	Red Jade Crab Apple	4-8
Malus 'Snowdrift'		
	Snowdrift Crab Apple	4-8
Malus x zumi 'Calocarpa'		
	Redbud Flowering Crab Apple	4-8
Melaleuca sp.	Melaleuca	9-10
Nerium oleander	Oleander	8-10
Oxydendrum arboreum		
	Sourwood	6-9
Prunus sp.	Flowering Fruit	3-10
Pyrus sp.	Pear	5-10
Robinia pseudoacacia		
	Black Locust	3-9
Sophora japonica		
	Japanese Pagoda Tree	5-8
Sorbus aucuparia		
	European Mountain Ash	2-7
Stewartia pseudocamellia		
	Japanese Stewartia	6-9
Styrax japonicus		
	Japanese Snowbell	6-9
Wisteria sp.	Wisteria	5-9

Yellow to Orange Blossoms

		Zones
Acacia baileyana	Bailey Acacia	9
Cassia excelsa		
	Crown of Gold Tree	10
Erythrina caffra		
	Kaffirboom Coral Tree	9-10
Koelreuteria sp.		
	Golden-Rain Tree	5-9
Laburnum x watereri 'Vossii'		
	Golden-Chain Tree	6-9
Nerium oleander	Oleander	8-10
Parkinsonia aculeata		
	Jerusalem Thorn	8-10
Sophora japonica		
	Japanese Pagoda Tree	5-8
Stewartia pseudocamellia		
	Japanese Stewartia	6-9

Purple to Blue Blossoms

		Zones
Bauhinia variegata		
	Purple Orchid Tree	9-10
Cercis sp.	Redbud	4-10
Jacaranda mimosifolia		
	Jacaranda	9-10
Lagerstroemia indica		
	Crape Myrtle	7-9
Magnolia x soulangiana		
	Saucer Magnolia	5-10
Malus	Flowering Crab Apple	4-8
Robinia x ambigua 'Idahoensis'		
	Idaho Locust	5-10
Wisteria sp.	Wisteria	5-9

Redbud *(Cercis canadensis)*

Flowering cherry *(Prunus sp.)*

Jacaranda *(Jacaranda mimosifolia)*

Pink Blossoms

		Zones
Aesculus x carnea 'Rosea'		
	Pink Horse Chestnut	5-9
Albizia julibrissin	Silk Tree	7-10
Cercis canadensis 'Pink Bud'		
	Pink Redbud	4-7
Cornus florida	Dogwood	5-9
Crataegus laevigata		
	English Hawthorn	5-8
Lagerstroemia indica		
	Crape Myrtle	7-9
Magnolia x soulangiana		
	Saucer Magnolia	5-10
Malus 'Radiant'		
	Flowering Crab Apple	4-8
Nerium oleander	Oleander	8-10
Prunus sp.	Flowering Fruit	3-10
Robinia x ambigua 'Idahoensis'		
	Idaho Locust	5-10

Red Blossoms

		Zones
Aesculus x carnea		
	Red Horse Chestnut	5-9
Callistemon sp.	Bottlebrush	8-10
Cercis canadensis 'Oklahoma'		
	Redbud	5-7
Cornus florida 'Cherokee Chief'		
	Dogwood	6-9
Crataegus laevigata		
	English Hawthorn	5-8
Erythrina sp.	Coral Tree	9-10
Eucalyptus ficifolia		
	Scarlet-Flowering Gum	9-10
Lagerstroemia indica		
	Crape Myrtle	7-9
Nerium oleander	Oleander	8-10

Beautiful Bark

Shaggy, shiny, mottled, peeling, or brightly colored bark adds interest during the off-season.

		Zones
Cercis sp.	Redbud	4-10
Cornus sp.	Dogwood	5-9
Eucalyptus sp.	Eucalyptus	7-10
Lagerstroemia indica		
	Crape Myrtle	7-9
Melaleuca sp.	Melaleuca	9-10
Prunus sp.	Flowering Fruit	3-10
Stewartia pseudocamellia		
	Japanese Stewartia	6-9

Beautiful Fall Color

These trees provide a reliable source of autumn color. Their foliage is as spectacular as their bloom, even in mild climates.

		Zones
Amelanchier sp.	Serviceberry	4-8
Cercis sp.	Redbud	4-10
Cornus sp.	Dogwood	5-9
Crataegus sp.	Hawthorn	5-9
Franklinia alatamaha		
	Franklin Tree	6-8
Lagerstroemia indica		
	Crape Myrtle	7-9
Liriodendron tulipifera		
	Tulip Tree	5-9
Oxydendrum arboreum		
	Sourwood	6-9
Pyrus calleryana	Callery Pear	5-9
Sophora japonica		
	Japanese Pagoda Tree	5-8
Sorbus aucuparia		
	European Mountain Ash	2-7
Stewartia pseudocamellia		
	Japanese Stewartia	6-9
Styrax japonicus		
	Japanese Snowbell	6-9

Summer-Flowering Trees

Summer-flowering trees bring color to the landscape long after the burst of bloom in spring.

		Zones
Albizia julibrissin	Silk Tree	7-10
Callistemon sp.	Bottlebrush	8-10
Cassia excelsa		
	Crown of Gold Tree	10
Catalpa sp.	Catalpa	5-10
Chionanthus virginicus		
	Fringe Tree	5-9
Erythrina crista-galli		
	Corkspur Coral Tree	9-10
Franklinia alatamaha		
	Franklin Tree	6-8
Jacaranda mimosifolia		
	Jacaranda	9-10
Koelreuteria sp.		
	Golden-Rain Tree	5-9
Lagerstroemia indica		
	Crape Mytle	7-9
Magnolia grandiflora		
	Southern Magnolia	7-10
Melaleuca sp.	Melaleuca	9-10
Nerium oleander	Oleander	8-10
Oxydendrum arboreum		
	Sourwood	6-9
Sophora japonica		
	Japanese Pagoda Tree	5-8
Stewartia pseudocamellia		
	Japanese Stewartia	6-9
Styrax japonicus		
	Japanese Snowbell	6-9

Crab apple *(Malus sp.)*

Flowering cherry *(Prunus sp.)*

Evergreen pear *(Pyrus kawakamii)*

Espalier

These flowering trees lend themselves to the time-honored practice of espalier. Espaliers are plants trained in a flat, vertical plane and tied to a wall or trellis. Branches are usually trained in geometric patterns. Espaliers can also be used as flowering hedges or garden dividers.

		Zones
Callistemon sp.	Bottlebrush	8-10
Citrus sp.	Citrus	9-10
Laburnum x watereri 'Vossii'		
	Golden-Chain Tree	6-9
Magnolia grandiflora		
	Southern Magnolia	7-10
Malus sp.	Crab Apple	4-8
Prunus sp.	Flowering Fruit	3-10
Pyrus sp.	Pear	5-10

Colorful Fruit

Brightly colored fruit can be a striking and long-lasting landscape attraction. Many of these fruits can also be brought to the kitchen table.

		Zones
Amelanchier sp.	Serviceberry	4-8
Citrus sp.	Citrus	9-10
Cornus sp.	Dogwood	5-9
Crataegus sp.	Hawthorn	5-9
Eucalyptus sp.	Eucalyptus	7-10
Koelreuteria sp.		
	Golden-Rain Tree	5-9
Malus sp.	Crab Apple	4-8
Prunus sp.	Flowering Fruit	3-10
Sorbus aucuparia		
	European Mountain Ash	2-7

Fragrant Blossoms

These trees are a blessing to the nose as well as to the eye. Some must be enjoyed up close, others will perfume an entire garden.

		Zones
Chionanthus virginicus		
	Fringe Tree	5-9
Citrus sp.	Citrus	9-10
Malus sp.	Crab Apple	4-8
Prunus sp.	Flowering Fruit	3-10
Robinia x ambigua 'Idahoensis'		
	Idaho Locust	5-10
Sophora japonica		
	Japanese Pagoda Tree	5-8
Styrax japonicus		
	Japanese Snowbell	6-9
Wisteria sp.	Wisteria	5-9

Winter Interest

Long-lasting, colorful fruit, interesting bark, and/or an attractive silhouette of bare branches make these trees welcome additions to the winter landscape.

		Zones
Amelanchier sp.	Serviceberry	4-8
Cercis sp.	Redbud	4-10
Citrus sp.	Citrus	9-10
Crataegus sp.	Hawthorn	5-9
Halesia carolina	Silver-Bell	5-8
Koelreuteria paniculata		
	Golden-Rain Tree	5-9
Lagerstroemia indica		
	Crape Myrtle	7-9
Malus sp.	Crab Apple	4-8
Oxydendrum arboreum		
	Sourwood	6-9
Stewartia pseudocamellia		
	Japanese Stewartia	6-9
Styrax japonicus		
	Japanese Snowbell	6-9

For Small Gardens and Patios

These are relatively small trees that fit neatly into areas of activity or limited space. Most are also appreciated best up close.

		Zones
Callistemon sp.	Bottlebrush	8-10
Cercis sp.	Redbud	4-10
Chionanthus virginicus		
	Fringe Tree	5-9
Citrus sp.	Citrus	9-10
Cornus sp.	Dogwood	5-9
Crataegus sp.	Hawthorn	5-9
Eucalyptus sp.	Eucalyptus	7-10
Halesia carolina	Silver-Bell	5-8
Lagerstroemia indica		
	Crape Myrtle	7-9
Magnolia x soulangiana		
	Saucer Magnolia	5-10
Magnolia stellata	Star Magnolia	5-10
Malus sp.	Crab Apple	4-8
Nerium oleander	Oleander	8-10
Oxydendrum arboreum		
	Sourwood	6-9
Prunus sp.	Flowering Fruit	3-10
Pyrus sp.	Pear	5-10
Stewartia pseudocamellia		
	Japanese Stewartia	6-9
Styrax japonicus		
	Japanese Snowbell	6-9
Wisteria sp.	Wisteria	5-9

Dogwood (*Cornus florida*)

Melaleuca (*Melaleuca sp.*)

Lemon-scented gum (*Eucalyptus sp.*)

To Garden Under

These trees have well-behaved roots and cast light enough shade to allow other plants to grow beneath them. Most are also excellent lawn trees.

		Zones
Albizia julibrissin	Silk Tree	7-10
Amelanchier sp.	Serviceberry	4-8
Cercis sp.	Redbud	4-10
Cornus sp.	Dogwood	5-9
Crataegus sp.	Hawthorn	5-9
Erythrina sp.	Coral Tree	9-10
Halesia carolina	Silver-Bell	5-8
Jacaranda mimosifolia		
	Jacaranda	9-10
Koelreuteria sp.		
	Golden-Rain Tree	5-9
Magnolia x soulangiana		
	Saucer Magnolia	5-10
Magnolia stellata	Star Magnolia	5-10
Prunus sp.	Flowering Fruit	3-10
Sophora japonica		
	Japanese Pagoda Tree	5-8
Sorbus aucuparia		
	European Mountain Ash	2-7
Styrax japonicus		
	Japanese Snowbell	6-9

For Wet Soils

Soggy, wet soils with poor drainage are deadly for most trees. The following trees can survive in wet soils. In areas with *extremely* poor drainage, consider planting in containers or raised beds.

		Zones
Eucalyptus citriodora		
	Lemon-Scented Gum	9-10
Magnolia grandiflora		
	Southern Magnolia	7-10
Melaleuca quinquenervia		
	Cajeput Tree	9-10
Pyrus sp.	Pear	5-10
Sophora japonica		
	Japanese Pagoda Tree	5-8

For the Seashore

Few flowering trees thrive under tough coastal conditions. The following trees do best. Those marked with an * are suited to the especially harsh conditions found on the Pacific Coast.

		Zones
*Amelanchier sp.**	Serviceberry	4-8
Crataegus crus-galli		
	Cockspur Thorn	5-9
*Erythrina caffra**		
	Kaffirboom Coral Tree	9-10
*Eucalyptus sp.**	Eucalyptus	7-10
Halesia monticola		
	Mountain Silver-Bell	5-8
Laburnum x watereri 'Vossii'		
	Golden-Chain Tree	6-9
Malus floribunda		
	Japanese Flowering Crab Apple	4-8
*Melaleuca quinquenervia**		
	Cajeput Tree	9-10
Robinia x ambigua 'Idahoensis'		
	Idaho Locust	5-10
Sorbus aucuparia		
	European Mountain Ash	2-7

Drought-Tolerant, Heat-Resistant

These trees are star performers for the hot, dry climates of desert areas or hot southern or western exposures around any home.

		Zones
Acacia baileyana	Bailey Acacia	9
Albizia julibrissin	Silk Tree	7-10
Callistemon citrinus		
	Lemon Bottlebrush	8-10
Cercis occidentalis		
	Western Redbud	7-10
Eucalyptus sp.	Eucalyptus	7-10
Koelreuteria paniculata		
	Golden-Rain Tree	5-9
Lagerstroemia indica		
	Crape Myrtle	7-9
Malus sp.	Crab Apple	4-8
Melaleuca sp.	Melaleuca	9-10
Nerium oleander	Oleander	8-10
Parkinsonia aculeata		
	Jerusalem Thorn	8-10
Robinia x ambigua 'Idahoensis'		
	Idaho Locust	5-10

Fast-Growing

These are trees you can rely on to grow rapidly.

		Zones
Acacia sp.	Acacia	9
Albizia julibrissin	Silk Tree	7-10
Callistemon sp.	Bottlebrush	8-10
Catalpa sp.	Catalpa	5-10
Eucalyptus sp.	Eucalyptus	7-10
Nerium oleander	Oleander	8-10
Parkinsonia aculeata		
	Jerusalem Thorn	8-10
Robinia x ambigua 'Idahoensis'		
	Idaho Locust	5-10

A Guide to Top-Rated Flowering Trees

The flowering trees described in this section were selected because of their top-rated growth performance and reliability. The majority of these plants are widely available in the climate zones to which they are adapted. A few trees that are not easily obtained are included because they were given special acclaim for their beauty and outstanding growth characteristics by many of the regional consultants who worked on this book. One of these unusual trees might be exactly the one you are looking for. Ask your nurseryman to obtain it for you.

Encyclopedia entries: The following descriptive entries are arranged alphabetically by the botanical name of the plant genus. For quick identification, the most widely used common names are shown in large, dark type immediately below the genus name.

Each entry includes the climate zones where the tree will grow, its potential height, and whether the tree is evergreen or deciduous. The growth habit, flower color and size, and other specific characteristics of the plant, such as leaf size and pattern, spread, bark texture, fruits, and berries are discussed. Information on soil requirements, preferred planting sites, long-term care, and any problems is given for each flowering tree. If cultivars or hybrids of interest to the home gardener are available, facts about those plants are given.

Planning helps: To help you plan how best to use these flowering trees around your home, entries discuss a variety of ways the plant can be used.

At left: Crab apple *(Malus sp.)* specimen trees add a woodland look to the landscape.

Catalpa *(Catalpa sp.)*

'Radiant' crab apple *(Malus sp.)*

Wisteria *(Wisteria sp.)*

Coral tree *(Erythrina sp.)*

Bailey acacias *(Acacia baileyana)* are colorful trees for dry climates.

Red horse chestnuts *(Aesculus x carnea)* are dramatic late spring-flowering trees for open areas. Blossoms shown below.

Acacia baileyana

Bailey Acacia

Zone: 9. To 20-30 feet.
Evergreen.

This fast-growing tree is widely planted in California. It is valued for its bright yellow, late winter flowers, drought tolerance, and ability to withstand neglect. Leaves are finely divided, fernlike. Prune lower limbs to obtain tree shape. Use in problem areas or where a quick effect is needed. Not a tree for small gardens.

Aesculus

Horse Chestnut, Buckeye

Thirteen species make up this genus of deciduous trees and shrubs native to east Asia, southeast Europe and North America. Several species have been selected as ornamentals for their large upright clusters of flowers, which may be red, pink, yellow, or white. Large leaves are divided into fanlike leaflets. Many species are subject to leaf scorch in hot, dry areas. Most horse chestnut trees cast dense shade.

Aesculus x carnea

Red Horse Chestnut

Zones: 5-9. To 40-70 feet.
Deciduous.

This dramatic tree is pyramidal when young, forming a rounded crown when mature. Grows at a slow to moderate rate. Stunning red to pink flowers in spikes to 10 inches tall appear in late spring. Grows best in moist, well-drained soil in full sunlight. Originated as a chance cross between *A. pavia* and *A. hippocastanum*.

This species is sometimes planted as a street tree to replace *A. hippocastanum* but is losing favor because it also is a litter-producing tree that drops flowers, nuts, and large leaves. Plant as a specimen tree in parks, large gardens, campuses, and other open areas where litter will not be a problem. Although a hybrid, red horse chestnut usually will come true from seed, producing either pink or red flowers.

A number of cultivars have been developed. 'Briottii' has large scarlet flowers. It is not hardy in Zone 5 except on sheltered sites. 'Rosea' has pink flowers.

Aesculus hippocastanum

Common Horse Chestnut

Zones: 4-8. To 50-75 feet.
Deciduous.

This is an upright oval to round tree with a medium growth rate. In mid-spring, white flowers blotched with red and yellow open in large upright showy spikes to 12 inches long. Produces shiny round nuts about an inch across. Native to the Balkans and brought to this country by the earliest settlers.

The horse chestnut is not as popular as it was a generation ago. It is a messy tree, dropping flowers, nuts, and leaves. Formerly considered a street tree, horse chestnut is now seldom planted for this purpose because of litter and pavement-breaking roots. Withstands city growing conditions and is tolerant of spray from deicing salts.

Grows best in moist, well-drained soil in full sunlight. Plant in parks and large open areas where litter will not be a problem. Some of its cultivars are favored. 'Alba' has pure white flowers; 'Baumannii' has double flowers and does not form nuts.

Horse chestnut is the famous chestnut of Paris. The nuts are poisonous, not edible.

Albizia julibrissin

Silk Tree, Mimosa

Zones: 7-10. To 25-35 feet.
Deciduous.

Pink flowers held above feathery foliage for two or more summer months highlight this wide-spreading, late-leafing tree. The light shade it casts provides an ideal environment for many low-growing plants and lawn grasses.

Silk tree, which is native from Iran to China, quickly forms multiple stems, developing a shape that is wider than tall with a flat top. The leaves are doubly compound with tiny leaflets that fold up on cool nights. The pink powder puff flowers, which consist of stamens rather than petals, open from July to September in northern areas and earlier in the South. Flowers bloom even on young trees. No fall foliage color develops. The flat 4- to 6-inch-long pods become brown and drop over a long period during fall and winter.

A tree for a sunny location, it will grow well in both poor and fertile soil as long as it is well drained. Silk tree tolerates considerable drought but grows best if kept moist. While most widely grown in mild climate areas, the botanical variety *rosea*, with bright pink flowers, grows well as far north as Boston (in Zone 6).

Mimosa wilt, which invades the root system, is serious in the South but is common in many other parts of the eastern United States. The first symptoms are yellow, wilted leaves, and tree death may follow within a year. There is no cure for this soil-borne fungus disease, but two cultivars, 'Charlotte' and 'Tryon', developed by the U.S. Department of Agriculture, are resistant to mimosa wilt and should be planted in problem areas.

Most silk trees are propagated by seed, so some variation in flower color and plant growth does occur. Flower color varies from almost white to dark pink. Root-cuttings 3 inches long, made from roots 1/3 inch in diameter and taken in early spring, will reproduce the original tree.

Amelanchier
Serviceberry, Shadbush
Zones: 4-8. To 20-50 feet. Deciduous.

Any one of four species, *A. alnifolia*, *A. canadensis*, *A. x grandiflora*, or *A. laevis*, are sold in nurseries. They are native to woodlands in various parts of the United States and are often confused with each other.

Silk trees *(Albizia julibrissin)* are wide-spreading and have feathery foliage that casts light shade.

Silk tree blossoms resemble powder puffs and are held well above the fernlike leaves during mid- and late summer.

Serviceberry *(Amelanchier alnifolia)*

Purple orchid tree *(Bauhinia variegata)*
Bottlebrush *(Callistemon sp.)*

Graceful clusters of white flowers are borne on bare branches in spring. The new foliage unfolds grayish or reddish, depending on the species, before becoming bright green, and turns shades of red and yellow in fall. Red berries are edible, favored by birds and lovers of jam and preserves. Plant in full sun or half-shade.

Bauhinia variegata (B. purpurea)

Purple Orchid Tree

Zones: 9-10. To 20-35 feet.
Deciduous.

This is a spectacular flowering tree for the mild winter climates of the Southwest and southern Florida. Produces a spectacular show of 2- to 3-inch purple flowers from midwinter to early spring. Usually grows as a multitrunk tree but can be trained to a single stem. Seed pods that follow blossoms are messy.

Callistemon

Bottlebrush

Callistemons are called bottlebrushes because the tightly-packed flowers, which are concentrated at the ends of the branches, are adorned with colorful stamens that resemble the bristles of a brush. These fast-growing Australian natives are used in sunny areas as a single plant specimen, as screens or informal hedges, or as an espalier on a wall or fence. Normally bushy plants, they can be pruned into the shape of a small tree.

Callistemon citrinus
Lemon Bottlebrush
Zones: 8-10. To 8-10 feet.
Evergreen.

The lemon bottlebrush forms a tall shrub unless the lower limbs are removed. By pruning, it is possible to develop a 20-foot or taller, round-headed tree in 10 years. Narrow foliage can vary from 1 to 3 inches long and is copper-colored as it emerges, becoming bright green with maturity. Bright red flower clusters are 2 to 6 inches long with 1-inch-long stamens. Seed capsules are ovoid and remain on the plant

for several years. Heaviest bloom is in the spring and summer but scattered flowering occurs throughout the year.

The common name of this species refers to the citrus odor emitted by the leaves when crushed. Much variability in leaf and flower cluster size occurs when this species is raised from seed. It is preferable to obtain plants grown by cuttings from select forms.

Lemon bottlebrush is drought-tolerant but grows best in a moist, well-drained soil. Alkaline and saline conditions are tolerated.

Callistemon viminalis
Weeping Bottlebrush
Zones: 8-10. To 20-30 feet.
Evergreen.

With pruning and periodic thinning, this bottlebrush can be developed into an attractive weeping tree of about 30 feet high and half as wide. It is best as a multitrunk specimen. Without thinning, the tree loses its attractive appearance and becomes top-heavy.

The 6-inch-long light green leaves are clustered at the ends of the long drooping branches. The bright red flowers open primarily in spring and early summer, but scattered blooms occur throughout the year.

This species requires frequent watering and is not a good tree for hot, windy, or dry locations. The varieties 'McCaskill' and 'Red Cascade' are more vigorous, with very showy flowers.

Cassia excelsa

Crown of Gold Tree

Zone: 10. To 25-30 feet.
Partially deciduous.

This is a fast-growing tree for southern California and mild areas of the Southwest desert. Large clusters of bright yellow flowers are borne in late summer and fall. Leaves are divided into many small leaflets. Prune after flowering. Water infrequently but deeply during the growing season.

Catalpa
Catalpa

This genus contains 13 species of deciduous or rarely evergreen trees native to North America and eastern Asia. Grown as ornamentals for their large clusters of showy flowers and dramatic foliage, catalpas offer flowers that are colored white, brownish pink, and yellow. Trees bloom in late spring or early summer. Most species will grow well in a wide range of soil types.

Catalpa bignonioides
Common Catalpa, Southern Catalpa
Zones: 5-10. To 50 feet.
Deciduous.

This broadly rounded, fast-growing tree has large heart-shaped leaves to 8 inches long with an unpleasant odor when bruised. Flowers in clusters to 10 inches long are white with 2 yellow stripes and brown spots. Mature trees, when in bloom, resemble a huge bouquet of flowers. Seed contained in long cylindrical pods gives the tree a local name of Indian bean tree.

A hardy tree able to withstand city smog and most other adverse conditions, this tree is native from Georgia to Florida and Mississippi but has proven hardy enough to plant farther north. In Zone 5 needs a sheltered site. Use as a lawn tree or as a specimen tree.

Cultivars include 'Aurea' with yellow leaves and 'Nana', a dwarf that is often grafted high to make umbrella-shaped trees with branches drooping to the ground.

Catalpa speciosa
Northern Catalpa, Western Catalpa
Zones: 5-10. To 100 feet.
Deciduous.

This is a pyramidal tree when young, becoming roundheaded as it matures. Leaves are up to 1 foot long and have less of an odor than the southern catalpa. Flowers are white with brown spots. The large clusters of flowers are very conspicuous and appear when most

Catalpas *(Catalpa sp.)* have large clusters of showy flowers. They are tough deciduous trees for difficult situations. Blossoms shown below.

25

Eastern redbuds *(Cercis canadensis)* are effective planted with an evergreen background. Blossoms shown below.

Fringe tree *(Chionanthus virginicus)*

trees have finished flowering. The seeds are contained in long brown beanlike pods to 20 inches long. Fallen pods make a messy cleanup job in spring.

This catalpa is hardier than its southern counterpart because it originated in the Midwest and is native from Southern Indiana and Iowa south to Arkansas and Texas. It will withstand hot summers and dry soil, and is tolerant of city environments. Western catalpa grows too large for small properties and should be planted in large open areas.

The caterpillar of the catalpa moth feeds on this tree's leaves. This large worm is good fish bait, and normally only fishermen notice it feeding.

Cercis
Redbud

This genus contains 8 species of small deciduous trees or shrubs growing in warm areas of the Northern Hemisphere.

Cercis canadensis
Eastern Redbud, Redbud
Zones: 4-7. To 25-40 feet.
Deciduous.

This tree has a short trunk and spreading branches with a rounded crown when young, and becomes flat-topped in later life. The spread of the crown is often equal to the height of the tree. The tree is frequently multistemmed, dividing into several trunks close to the ground if it is not trained.

Dainty, pink to purplish-pink, pealike flowers, clustered along the twigs and branches, appear in early spring before the leaves. The heart-shaped leaves are reddish purple when first unfolding, soon becoming a dark green color that looks attractive all summer. An added plus is the yellow autumn foliage.

Redbud can be grown in full sun or light shade. In the wild it usually grows as an understory tree in hardwood forests in moist soils of valleys and slopes. It is not too fussy about soil pH and will grow in either acid or alkaline soils providing they are

not too extreme, but redbud dislikes wet soils with poor drainage. Best growth is made on deep, fertile, moist soils with good drainage.

Redbud has been used as an ornamental for many years in the United States. George Washington transplanted some from the woods into his garden at Mount Vernon. Redbuds are very effective as accent trees, set in group plantings, or planted in shrub borders. They are lovely naturalized in open woodlands and they are excellent patio trees especially attractive against a light-colored background. The tree begins to bloom when quite young.

A number of cultivars and varieties have been selected. The variety *texensis* is adapted to Texas; *alba* has white flowers. Cultivars 'Wither's Pink Charm' and 'Pink Bud' have pure pink flowers and 'Oklahoma' has dark red flowers. These forms are slightly less cold hardy than the species.

Cercis occidentalis
Western Redbud
Zones: 7-10. To 10-18 feet.
Deciduous.

Western redbud is a good tree for the dry areas of the western United States. It tolerates poor soils and drought. Smaller than eastern redbud, the plant usually grows in multitrunk form with a spread equal to its height. Small magenta spring flowers are followed by interesting seed pods that last on the branches after foliage turns yellow or red in fall, and drops.

Chionanthus virginicus
Fringe Tree
Zones: 5-9. To 30 feet.
Deciduous.

Fringe tree is a large, spreading, open shrub that can be trained into an attractive tree. Clusters of fragrant white flowers to 8 inches long appear in late spring or early summer. Blossoms are dainty, with narrow fringelike petals. Use in group plantings, as an accent, or as a transition tree. Full sun or partial shade. Deep, well-drained, acid, loamy soil. Fringe tree tolerates city conditions.

Citrus
Citrus

Citrus trees provide colorful, edible fruit, fragrant white flowers, and evergreen foliage to shade or screen in warm climates. Heights listed are for trees grafted on standard rootstocks and will be 40 to 50 percent shorter on dwarf rootstocks. In colder areas, citrus on dwarf rootstock can be grown outdoors in tubs in warm weather if they are brought inside before it becomes cold. These natives of Southeast Asia need full sun or partial shade and fertile, well-drained soil. They require regular watering.

Basically all citrus are hardy throughout Zones 9 and 10, but there are differences between citrus types.

Citrus
Calamondin

Zones: 9-10. To 15-25 feet.
Evergreen.

Upright growth habit, fine texture, cold hardiness, and attractive fruit make this *Citrus* top-rated for landscape use. The small red-orange fruits peel easily, revealing orange flesh. When sweetened, the juice makes a good drink. Fruit holds on the tree almost year-round.

Citrus
'Marsh Seedless' Grapefruit

Zones: 9-10. To 20-25 feet.
Evergreen.

'Marsh Seedless', the white grapefruit of the supermarket, grows on a tall, vigorous, spreading tree with glossy, deep green leaves. Clusters of large yellow fruits show well. A long, hot season is needed for top quality. Ripening takes 12 to 14 months in hot climates and up to 18 months in cooler areas. Fruit holds well on the tree.

Citrus
'Redblush' Grapefruit

Zones: 9-10. To 20-25 feet.
Evergreen.

'Redblush', a sport of 'Marsh Seedless', is the standard red-fleshed supermarket variety. The vigorous tree has the same tall, spreading

Fringe trees *(Chionanthus virginicus)* are lovely plants with dainty fragrant blossoms. They can be trained to form handsome small trees for a variety of landscape uses.

Calamondins *(Citrus sp.)* are small trees that make colorful container plants, indoors or out.

Colorful grapefruits *(Citrus sp.)* are borne toward the outside of the tree.

'Washington' navel orange trees *(Citrus sp.)* bear bright-colored fruits from November to January.

habit, and the fruit is of excellent quality. The crimson-blushed skin gives a different ornamental effect. Red flesh develops under hot growing conditions but not in coastal areas.

Citrus
'Nagami' Dwarf Kumquat
Zones: 9-10. To 6-8 feet.
Evergreen.

Bright orange fruits are oval, about 1 inch long. Excellent for eating fresh (the edible rind is sweet, flesh is tart), for marmalade, jelly, candies, or preserved whole. Tree is hardier than most citrus, to 18°F. Very productive and ornamental.

Citrus
'Eureka' Lemon
Zones: 9-10. To 15-20 feet.
Evergreen.

'Eureka' has dark green leaves and a somewhat open habit. It is frost sensitive but in suitable climates flowering and fruiting is almost year-round, providing continuous fragrance, bright yellow color, and an ample supply of fruit. Best picked soon after fruit turns yellow. Fruit left on the tree too long loses flavor.

Citrus
'Improved Meyer' Lemon
Zones: 9-10. To 8-15 feet.
Evergreen.

Smaller and more spreading than other lemons, this is one of the most cold hardy citrus. Flowers and ripe fruit appear throughout the year, making a pretty show. It is good in tubs and home orchards. This is a virus-free form of 'Meyer' lemon. The fruit is sweeter than other lemons.

Citrus
'Bearss' Lime
Zones: 9-10. To 15-20 feet.
Evergreen.

This roundheaded tree has dense vigorous growth and does not have a high heat requirement for fruit development. It is identical to the Tahitian or Persian lime and is top-rated because of its beautiful habit.

Fruits, which are about the size of small lemons, are pale yellow at maturity. Pale greenish-yellow flesh has true lime flavor but lacks the aroma of the Mexican or key lime. The ripening period is from June to March depending on location.

Citrus
'Dancy' Mandarin
Zones: 9-10. To 15-25 feet.
Evergreen.

'Dancy', grown commercially in Florida, is the leading Christmas tangerine variety. Top-rated for home gardens, 'Dancy' is an erect tree of vigorous habit, having few thorns. The small to medium-sized, easy-peeling, red-orange fruits are held to the outside of the tree, making a good show. In cool areas they ripen in spring.

Citrus
'Kara' Mandarin
Zones: 9-10. To 15-25 feet.
Evergreen.

This is a nearly thornless tree with a spreading, open habit. Grows at a moderate rate. The large dark green leaves tend to droop. Orange, medium-large fruits peel easily and hold up fairly well but become puffy. Ripening from March to June, the best quality comes from interior regions, except desert areas.

Citrus
'Owari' Satsuma Mandarin
Zones: 9-10. To 8-10 feet.
Evergreen.

Forming a small to medium-sized tree, this is the hardiest mandarin variety. Almost seedless fruits are a medium size. Ripens early, from October to December. Fruit does not hold well on tree; pick when ripe. Yields are poor in desert climates.

Citrus
'Chinotto' Sour Orange
Zones: 9-10. To 10-15 feet.
Evergreen.

'Chinotto' is a decorative small round tree with closely spaced flowers and leaves. The small, flattened, easy-to-peel, deep orange fruits are used for making candy as well as jellies and preserves. The fruit holds well and ripens from November to March.

Citrus
'Valencia' Orange
Zones: 9-10. To 20-30 feet. Evergreen.

The standard juice orange 'Valencia' is a vigorous-growing globe-shaped tree. Depending on the climate, fruits of this thin-skinned variety begin to ripen sometime between February and April, with a long harvest period. Fruit quality is better at late harvest dates.

Citrus
'Washington' Navel Orange
Zones: 9-10. To 15-20 feet. Evergreen.

The standard navel orange has a round-topped, slightly drooping habit with heavy, dark green foliage. Large, easy-to-peel fruits colored deep orange ripen from November to January, but hold well without losing quality.

Citrus
'Algerian' Tangerine, 'Clementine' Mandarin
Zones: 9-10. To 14-16 feet. Evergreen.

This is an attractive small to medium-sized tree with a weeping form and dense, dark green leaves. The small to medium-sized, easy-to-peel, red-orange fruits ripen from November to February but hold well on the tree. Fruits held toward the outside of the canopy are showy and attractive.

Cornus
Dogwood
There are 40 to 45 species in this genus of mostly deciduous shrubs and small trees. There is a wide range of sizes among the species, from the ground-hugging bunchberry (*C. canadensis*), which may be 9 inches high, to the giant mountain dogwood (*C. nuttallii*), which may be 75 feet tall. Most dogwoods require

Dwarf citrus *(Citrus sp.)* are usually 40 to 50 percent smaller than standard trees, and are much easier to care for.

'Algerian' tangerine *(Citrus sp.)*

29

Pruned dogwoods *(Cornus florida)* form a solid mass of bloom.

Japanese dogwoods *(Cornus kousa)* bloom for a month in early summer. Blossoms shown below.

a fertile, slightly acid, moist but well-drained soil. Some need shade, others full sunlight, while some can grow equally well in either shade or full sun. These ornamental trees are grown for their spectacular spring floral display.

Cornus florida
Flowering Dogwood.
Zones: 5-9. To 20-40 feet.
Deciduous.

Probably more people are familar with this tree than with any other flowering tree. Having mostly horizontal, spreading branches, these trees usually develop a flat-topped crown that can be wider than high at maturity.

Large white flower bracts surround clusters of small greenish-white or yellow flowers in the center. The bracts, up to two inches in diameter, are the most conspicuous part of the flower. Flowers are borne profusely in early spring before the leaves emerge.

In late summer and early fall the nearly 1/2-inch-long glossy red fruits add color until eaten by the birds. Fall leaf color is reddish purple and appears early. The bark on the trunk and larger branches breaks up into an unusual checkered pattern resembling the back of an alligator. This bark, together with the graceful branching habit, gives dogwood a beautiful winter appearance and handsome silhouette.

Wild flowering dogwoods are usually found growing around the edges of woodlands or in open woods where they receive partial shade at least part of the day. Nature does not use this dogwood as a pioneer species on open bare soils where they would be subjected to winds and full sunlight all day. The best growing sites should duplicate where they grow naturally.

One of the biggest problems is lawn-mower disease. Bumping the bases of the trunks with the lawn-mower causes wounds or kills patches of bark; the wounds are then frequently invaded by dogwood borers, hastening the decline of the trees. Poor growing conditions will also attract this insect.

Herbicides should be used with caution near dogwoods, because the trees can be severely damaged or killed by picking up these chemicals through the root system or by wind-drift from nearby areas.

One of the best of the native ornamentals, dogwood fits into many landscape locations. Use as a specimen tree, a patio tree, in group plantings, and at the corners of buildings. Many varieties and cultivars have been selected that have superior features or special uses.

Occasionally a red- or pink-flowered form occurs naturally. Many of these have been propagated so there is a wide range of colors from light pink to dark red. Unfortunately most are from southern states and are not as hardy as the species. They should be planted in Zone 6 and farther south. Red and pink selections include: 'Rubra', pink to red; 'Cherokee Chief', red bracts; and 'Cherokee Princess', light pink bracts.

'Fragrant Cloud' has been selected for its fragrance and abundant white flowers. 'Cloud Nine' is a small tree with huge quantities of flowers. Two with variegated leaves include 'First Lady' with white-and-green leaves and 'Rainbow' with yellow-and-green leaves. 'New Hampshire' is especially hardy and can be grown in Zone 4, pushing the natural growing area farther north.

Cornus kousa
Japanese Dogwood
Zones: 6-9. To 20 feet.
Deciduous.

Vase-shaped when young, this tree becomes rounded with a distinct stratified appearance as it ages. Similar in many ways to *C. florida*, but slightly less cold hardy, it blooms later in the season so is valued for extending the spring floral show. Flower bracts are pointed rather than being rounded or notched. The large, showy, spherical fruits are an inch in diameter and somewhat resemble raspberries.

Chinese dogwood, the cultivar 'Chinensis', has extremely large white flower heads, up to 5 or 6 inches across, that remain in good condition for up to a month. It flowers more profusely than the species. Grows 10 to 12 feet tall trained as either a small tree or shrub.

The flower bracts of cultivar 'Summer Stars' may last up to six weeks in warm weather, long after other varieties have faded. It is also somewhat drought-resistant.

Japanese dogwood has the same landscape uses as the flowering dogwood.

Crataegus
Hawthorn

A large genus of mostly deciduous plants, *Crataegus* contains more named species than any other native genus—more than 1,100 have been described. With few exceptions they are dense and twiggy, armed with thorns up to 3 inches long. Tree-forms vary from 15 to 35 feet tall. They are used for their ornamental white, pink, or red blooms in spring and for the red to orange fruit that ripens in late summer or early fall. The berries often remain on the trees all winter. Leaves are glossy green on most species. Many have brilliant red to orange fall coloration, and during winter their wide-spreading branches make a picturesque silhouette.

Hawthorns should not be used where thorns are objectionable or dangerous to passersby. Because pruning is tolerated they can be developed into trespass-proof hedges. They also make beautiful specimen trees on lawns, around buildings, and as screens.

Thornless, or essentially thornless, cultivars such as Ohio pioneer dotted hawthorn (*C. punctata* 'Ohio Pioneer') and thornless cockspur hawthorn (*C. crus-galli inermis*) have been selected. Care should be exercised to plant types that are resistant to fireblight, a disease that can be devastating in some areas of the country.

English hawthorns *(Crataegus laevigata)* are graceful flowering trees providing colorful blooms, bright berries, and fall color.

English hawthorn *(Crataegus laevigata)*

English hawthorn *(Crataegus laevigata)*

Natal coral tree *(Erythrina humeana)*

Hawthorns are tough plants able to withstand the adverse growing conditions of a city. They are difficult to transplant but once established they are long-lived. Although best growth is made in rich loamy soils, they can grow almost equally well on slightly acid or slightly alkaline soils and can survive on poor soils. Sunny locations are a must for maximum development of flowers and fruit. To avoid excessive growth, hawthorns should be grown on sites that are on the dry side.

Crataegus crus-galli
Cockspur Thorn
Zones: 5-9. To 18-25 feet.
Deciduous.

This is a tough American native able to withstand climate extremes and heavy pruning. Flowers are white. Fruit is long-lasting and red. Glossy, dark green leaves turn orangish red in fall. Useful as a hedge. The variety *inermis* is thornless.

Crataegus laevigata (C. oxyacantha)
English Hawthorn
Zones: 5-8. To 18-25 feet.
Deciduous.

This tree is widely used in Europe as a hedge plant. The species is quite variable, with white, pink, or red flowers. Unreliable fall color. Does poorly in summer heat and humidity due to susceptibility to fungal leaf spot disease.

Varieties that are planted more often than the species include: 'Paul's Scarlet' with beautiful clusters of rose-red flowers but no fruit; 'Autumn Glory' with single white flowers and large long-lasting red fruit. 'Crimson Cloud', the most disease-resistant and best for hot, humid eastern climates, bears bright crimson flowers with white centers followed by long-lasting red fruit; thorny.

Crataegus x lavallei
Lavelle Hawthorn
Zones: 5-8. To 20 feet.
Deciduous.

Glossy green leaves turn bronzy-red in fall. White flowers. Red fruit. Thorny.

Crataegus phaenopyrum
Washington Hawthorn
Zones: 5-9. To 30 feet.
Deciduous.

This commonly planted native species has stood the test of time—it's been grown for scores of years in the inner city. At first columnar in form, Washington hawthorn soon develops a round head. The numerous sharp thorns are 3 inches long. Abundant white flowers in late spring, followed by a heavy set of 1/4-inch scarlet fruits, can be expected almost every year. In the fall the foliage turns scarlet to orange.

Erythrina
Coral Tree

These thorny deciduous trees and shrubs (some almost evergreen) are grown for their brilliant flowers, which often develop on bare branches. Leaves are divided into 3 leaflets. The strong trunk and branch structure give a sculptured appearance with or without leaves. They do best in full sun in well-drained soils but need watering in the dry season.

Erythrina caffra
Kaffirboom Coral Tree
Zones: 9-10. To 25-40 feet.
Deciduous.

This South African native is renowned for its spectacular flowers that appear on bare branches during the winter. A fast-growing tree with stout, irregular branches, it grows wider than tall. All the young growth is thorny (even the stems of the dark green leaves have thorns), but old limbs usually are not. Leaves drop in January. New leaves develop in March, forming a dense leafy canopy.

Large clusters of 2-inch, deep orange to bright vermillion, tubular flowers bloom during February. The red seeds contained in the 4-inch, semiwoody seed pods that follow flowering are poisonous to animals and people. This species is excellent for planting in seaside locations, where few flowering trees perform well.

Erythrina coralloides
Naked Coral Tree
Zones: 9-10. To 25-30 feet.
Deciduous.

Grown for its striking branch structure and fiery red flowers. Blossoms cluster like pinecones at the tips of the bare, twisted stems from March until May. A good shade tree, it grows about as wide as it is tall, but can be controlled by pruning.

Erythrina crista-galli
Cockspur Coral Tree
Zones: 9-10. To 15-20 feet.
Deciduous.

A small multistemmed tree that becomes as wide as it is tall in frost-free areas. Prized for its birdlike pinkish-red flowers, which are produced in repeated flushes from spring to fall after the leaves develop.

Erythrina humeana
Natal Coral Tree
Zones: 9-10. To 20-30 feet.
Usually deciduous, but sometimes almost evergreen.

Flowering starts when natal coral tree is only 3 feet tall. Bright orange flowers appear continuously from late August to late November and are held well above the dark green foliage.

Eucalyptus
Eucalyptus

Eucalyptus are vigorous-growing trees and shrubs native to Australia. They provide evergreen foliage, light shade, wind protection, and attractive bark and flowers. Most eucalyptus are drought-tolerant but the growth rate of new plants will be increased with some irrigation. A mulch to keep down weeds and reduce evaporation will also increase growth of young trees. Good drainage is essential. Eucalyptus are free of insect pests. Because they were imported as seed, the pests that chew their leaves in Australia were left behind. Also, eucalyptus are not bothered by foliage disease.

Kaffirboom coral trees *(Erythrina caffra)* are low and wide-spreading, ideal for lining parkways or wide avenues.

Cockspur coral tree *(Erythrina crista-galli)*

Roundheaded scarlet-flowering gums (*Eucalyptus ficifolia*) are good for street planting. Blossom shown below.

Franklin tree (*Franklinia alatamaha*)

Eucalyptus cinerea
Silver-Dollar Tree
Zones: 8-10. To 20-50 feet.
Evergreen.

One of the smaller species whose silver-blue foliage is excellent for cutting. The whitish bark and cream-colored flowers are very attractive.

Eucalyptus citriodora
Lemon-Scented Gum
Zones: 9-10. To 50-100 feet.
Evergreen.

Lemon-scented, long-pointed leaves are the major attraction of this slender, fast-growing, high-branching tree. It has white to pinkish bark and white flowers that open in October.

Eucalyptus ficifolia
Scarlet-Flowering Gum
Zones: 9-10. To 30-60 feet.
Evergreen.

The winner among the eucalyptus for floral display is this medium-sized, roundheaded tree with thick, dark green leaves. Large clusters of 1-1/2 inch, red flowers cover the tree in August. Large seed capsules develop after flowering.

Eucalyptus gunnii
Cider Gum
Zones: 7-10. To 40-75 feet.
Evergreen.

A cold-tolerant species that makes a good shade, windbreak, or screening tree. The small, blue-gray foliage of young trees is good for cutting. White flowers open in April.

Eucalyptus polyanthemos
Red Gum, Silver-Dollar Gum
Zones: 8-10. To 20-60 feet.
Evergreen.

A medium-sized tree, often multi-stemmed and low-branched. Oval grayish-blue leaves contrast with the rough, brown or gray bark. Small creamy flowers open in March.

Eucalyptus viminalis
Manna Gum
Zones: 8-10. To 150 feet.
Evergreen.

This fast-growing, white-barked tree has an open habit with weeping branchlets. The willowlike pale green leaves and small white flowers, which bloom from June to September, are very attractive. Manna gum grows best in good soil, but will grow in poor soil.

Franklinia alatamaha
Franklin Tree
Zones: 6-8. To 20-30 feet.
Deciduous.

A small pyramidal tree or shrub. White flowers with yellow centers appear in late summer. Plant in moist, acid, well-drained soil with ample organic matter, in partial shade or sun. Best in protected sites. Leaves turn orange to red in fall with best coloration in full sun. Use as a specimen tree.

Halesia carolina
Silver-Bell
Zones: 5-8. To 30-40 feet.
Deciduous.

Silver-bell is pyramidal in youth, becoming a roundheaded tree or shrub. Petite (1/2-inch), white, bell-shaped flowers hang in graceful clusters in spring as the leaves appear. Oval, finely toothed leaves turn yellow in fall. Plant in rich, moist, well-drained, acid soil in sun or partial shade. Use as a lawn tree, or an accent in woodland borders. A similar species, *H. monticola*, grows to 100 feet.

Jacaranda mimosifolia
Jacaranda
Zones: 9-10. To 25-40 feet.
Deciduous to semievergreen.

This spectacular tree from Argentina and Brazil, sometimes sold as *J.*

acutifolia or *J. ovalifolia,* is grown in subtropical areas for its fernlike foliage and large blue flowers.

Jacaranda is open growing with a shape varying from upright with a thick trunk, to irregular with several trunks. Width of the tree is 2/3 to 3/4 its height. The fernlike leaves, up to 18 inches long, are finely divided, each having 18 to 48 oblong leaflets 1/4 to 1/3 inch long. Jacaranda's leaves fall in February to March and new leaves may develop quickly, or the tree may stay bare until flowering time.

Flowering is usually in spring, but can be anytime between April and September. The slightly fragrant, showy, blue flowers are arranged in 8-inch-tall, loose clusters of 40 to 90 tubular flowers, each 2 inches long and 1-1/2 inches wide. There are varieties with white and orchid-pink flowers. The white-flowered form usually has more lush foliage and a longer blooming period, but fewer flowers. Woody, oval seed capsules, 1 to 2 inches across and 3/8 inch thick, are decorative in arrangements.

Young plants are damaged below 25°F but often grow back after freezing, forming multistemmed plants. They become hardier after mature hardwood develops. Propagation is by seed. Jacarandas grow best in acid, sandy soils, but will grow in other soils. Regular irrigation is necessary to maintain balanced growth. Too little water stunts the plant, while too much water results in excessive soft growth. Jacaranda does not flower well when exposed to cool ocean breezes and is best planted in warmer areas sheltered from strong winds.

When viewed from above, as from a hillside house or a high deck, jacaranda is at its most spectacular, but is also very attractive viewed from ground level. Useful as a garden or street tree, because branches at 6 to 10 feet in height are easy to develop. As street trees, jacarandas should be planted 40 feet apart. Staking and pruning may be necessary to develop the desired form for this use.

The intense flower color of jacaranda trees *(Jacaranda mimosifolia)* provides visual excitement in the landscape.

Silver-bell *(Halesia carolina)*

Chinese flame trees (*Koelreuteria bipinnata*) are top-rated lawn and shade trees.

Golden-rain trees (*Koelreuteria paniculata*) produce papery, lanternlike fruit after summer blossoms.

Golden-chain trees (*Laburnum x watereri* 'Vossii') bear wisterialike flowers in late spring.

Koelreuteria
Koelreuteria

These medium-sized, deciduous trees are grown for their large clusters of yellow flowers, showy seed pods, and large divided leaves. They are deep-rooted and are excellent for use as street, shade, or patio trees.

Koelreuteria bipinnata
Chinese Flame Tree
Zones: 5-9. To 20-40 feet. Deciduous.

This wide-spreading native of China grows at a slow to moderate rate, eventually becoming flat-topped. The compound leaves measure up to 2 feet long and nearly as wide and have many oval, medium green leaflets that turn yellow before dropping in December. Large clusters of bright yellow flowers with purple-spotted bases are held above the foliage in summer. Two-inch-long, triangular, papery capsules, colored orange, red, or salmon, add interest during summer and fall.

Chinese flame tree grows in most soils that are well drained, but needs some irrigation. Staking and pruning are needed to develop a high head.

Koelreuteria paniculata
Golden-Rain Tree
Zones: 5-9. To 20-35 feet. Deciduous.

A native of Korea and China, golden-rain tree is more cold hardy than *K. bipinnata*, but the wood is weak and limbs may break during snow and ice storms. Grows at a moderate rate in an open pattern, spreading as wide as it is tall. Leaves are up to 18 inches long with 12 to 18 deeply cut, bright green leaflets. Yellow fall leaf color is not outstanding. Loose, triangular flower clusters with masses of small flowers open in July and August. Flower color varies from pale green-yellow to deep yellow. Bright green, inflated papery seed pods, which become tan or brown when mature, follow the flowers. They resemble Chinese paper lanterns.

Grows best in fertile, well-drained, moist soil in full sun, but adapts well to poorer and drier soils. Tolerates air pollution, drought, heat, wind, and alkaline soil.

Large trees do not transplant well because of their deep root systems. Many seedlings develop near the tree, causing a weed problem. The fungus necteria canker, identified by coral-colored spots on dead wood, is the only troublesome disease.

Laburnum x watereri 'Vossii'
Golden-Chain Tree
Zones: 6-9. To 25-30 feet. Deciduous.

'Vossii' is a superior form of golden-chain tree that occurs naturally in Europe. Like all laburnums, it is grown chiefly for its showy yellow flowers that hang in clusters like wisteria blossoms. The species *L. x watereri* is a hybrid between *L. alpinum* and *L. anagyroides*. Its flowers are larger and deeper yellow than either parent, and its flower clusters are longer, up to 20 inches. All plant parts, especially the seeds, of laburnum are poisonous. However, seed often does not set on 'Vossii', so it is less likely to be a hazard than the species.

Golden-chain tree is best planted in an area where its spring bloom can be appreciated, but where it blends into the landscape the rest of the year, since it is an unassuming tree when not in bloom. Laburnum is not bothered by any pests other than mites.

Grow in moist soil in full sun or partial shade. Protect from strong winds.

Lagerstroemia indica
Crape Myrtle
Zones: 7-9. To 10-30 feet. Deciduous.

The profusion of colorful flowers for several summer months makes this one of the best small flowering trees for patio, specimen, or street tree use. Native to China, crape myrtle is grown throughout the world in warm temperate areas. Normally a small tree, shrub types useful for espaliers, foundation plantings, shrub borders, and hedges have been bred.

A vase shape develops if pruned to several stems, while a round head forms if pruned to a single stem. The outstanding gray or light brown bark peels in patches revealing a pink inner bark, which adds interest all year long if the lower branches are removed. The glossy, dark green leaves are 1/2-inch long and 3/4 to 1-1/4 inches wide. Fall color depends on the climate and variety but leaves can turn yellow, orange, or brilliant red. Clusters of ruffled flowers, 6 to 15 inches tall, are crinkled like crepe paper and open from July to September. Individual flowers are up to 1-1/2 inches across and have 5 to 8 petals. Colors are white, pink, rose, red, lavender, and purple. A variety with white-edged petals, called 'Peppermint Lace', is a recent development.

Many selections are available trained in tree or shrub form. White varieties are: 'White', 'Glendora White'. Pinks: 'Pink Ruffles', 'Rosea'. Rose-pink flowers bordered with white: 'Peppermint Lace'. Reds: 'Durant Red', 'Watermelon Red'. Purples: 'Majestic Orchid', 'Select Purple'. The 'Petite' series is shrubby, with plants growing 5 to 7 feet tall in a full color range. 'Crape Myrtlettes', an even smaller-growing group, is raised from seed.

Crape myrtle should be planted in full sun and grows well in a wide variety of soils. A drought-resistant plant, it should be watered infrequently but thoroughly. Chlorosis may develop in alkaline soils but can be corrected by the application of iron. Mildew can be a serious problem in humid or cool areas. It can be controlled by fungicides. A group of mildew-tolerant varieties, with the names of Indian tribes, has been developed at the U.S. National Arboretum. Varieties in different flower colors and with colorful bark are available.

Crape myrtles *(Lagerstroemia indica)* live up to their reputation as one of the most colorful summer-flowering trees and make decorative street plantings.

Crape myrtle *(Lagerstroemia indica)*

Tulip trees *(Liriodendron tulipifera)* are large deciduous trees for open areas.

Tulip tree *(Liriodendron tulipifera)*

Liriodendron tulipifera
Yellow Poplar, Tulip Tree

Zones: 5-9. To 80-100 feet. Deciduous.

The tallest native hardwood in the eastern United States, yellow poplars in virgin forests reach heights of 200 feet with 12-foot diameters. Trees develop a long straight trunk with a narrow crown that becomes spreading with age. Yellow-green leaves are lyre-shaped and 5 to 6 inches long and wide. Leaves turn yellow in autumn.

When 10 to 12 years old, trees begin to bear tulip-shaped flowers. The greenish-yellow flowers, with orange stripes at the bases, appear after the leaves have developed. Flowers, from 1-1/2 to 2 inches long, are borne high in the tree and are inconspicuous unless one looks for them. As much as a teaspoonful of nectar is produced in a flower, and when in bloom, trees are alive with honeybees. The clean-looking, furrowed bark resembles that of a true poplar, accounting for one of the common names.

Yellow poplar needs lots of growing room. Used in open areas, such as parks, golf courses, large properties, and on spacious lawns, it makes an ideal shade, specimen, background, or skyline tree. Plant the cultivar 'Fastigiata', a small upright tree reaching 35 feet, on small-sized properties.

Tulip trees should not be planted near parking lots or patios, as drip of nectar, and honeydew from aphids and other sucking insects, can mar the finish of parked cars or paved surfaces. A deep, wide-spreading root system may interfere with water and sewer lines if planted too close. The wood is somewhat brittle, and occasionally branches break off during ice and wind storms, making it unwise to plant this tree close to buildings or utility lines.

A fast-growing tree on good sites, in northern areas the tulip tree may increase in height up to 3 feet a year when young, then slows down, averaging a foot a year when 60 years old. In southern mountains its growth rate may reach half again this average. Natural growth is best in the deep, rich, moist, but well-drained, loamy soils found in the coves of the southern mountains. Prefers a slightly acid soil. Requires a good supply of moisture, becoming somewhat stunted on dry sites. Should be planted in full sun.

Magnolia
Magnolia

This large genus has over 85 species of evergreen and deciduous trees and shrubs native to warm temperate and tropical regions in North America and Asia. Evergreen species are not hardy in the North. Magnolias are valued for their large flowers. Some species bear among the largest of tree flowers; blooms may be up to a foot in diameter. Flowers of many species are fragrant and colors may be white, yellow, red, or purplish red.

Fruits are usually quite conspicuous, often shaped like cucumbers. Ripe seeds attached to long silken threads are released and hang for several days before falling to the ground. Leaves are quite coarse and stiff.

Most magnolias do best in fertile, well-drained loamy soils that hold ample moisture. Some thrive in peaty soils if they are well aerated. Mixing peat or compost in the backfill when planting is recommended. A compost mulch spread underneath the area covered by the crown is beneficial when applied in spring and fall. Magnolias should not be transplanted after they become established, because injury to large roots can be very damaging.

Magnolias should be planted at least 40 feet away from other trees or buildings, allowing room for full plant development. Trees with large leaves are not suitable for windy sites, because winds can whip the leaves about, tearing and shredding them until they become unsightly.

Pruning must be done during the growing season, because dormant trees do not heal their wounds easily. If possible, confine pruning to young plants and small branches. Wounds made by removing large branches do not heal well, and decay can set in.

Magnolia grandiflora
Southern Magnolia
Zones: 7-10. To 80-100 feet.
Evergreen.

Southern magnolia is native to the coastal plain from North Carolina to Florida to southeast Texas. Trees can grow to 100 feet tall with crown spreads of 30 to 50 feet. Shape varies according to site and variability of seedlings. Forest-grown trees can have trunks clear of branches for 40 feet, while open-grown trees may have their lower branches touching the ground. Forest-grown trees, 60 feet to 80 feet tall and 2 to 3 feet in diameter, are 80 to 120 years old.

Flowers, carried throughout summer and fall, are white, very fragrant, and may be a foot in diameter when fully opened. Large leaves, 5 to 8 inches long, are thick and leathery, shiny green above and a fuzzy rust color beneath. Foliage is dense and casts a heavy shadow. When grown from seed, the tree will probably bear flowers in 15 to 20 years. Grafted trees may begin blooming 2 to 3 years after planting in open soil.

Since this magnolia can grow into a large tree with a wide-spreading crown, it is not suitable for small gardens but should be planted where there is enough space for potential development. Use as a specimen tree on the lawn, in the background, or in parks. Street tree plantings can be made, but the tree should be set far enough back from traffic so the soft tender bark will not be injured. Some shade is acceptable when young, but full sunlight is required as the tree becomes older.

Saucer magnolia trees *(Magnolia x soulangiana)* have bold-textured blossoms, and cast a graceful shadow pattern.

Star magnolias *(Magnolia stellata)* are covered with fragrant flowers in early spring before leaves unfold.

Southern magnolia (*Magnolia grandiflora*)

While southern magnolias are best adapted to Zones 7 to 10, hardy strains are continually being developed and tested, with the hope of extending the planting of this tree farther north. Some hardy strains have survived into Zone 6 on protected sites. Leaves will often be killed at temperatures of 10° to 15°F. Some cultivars with special characteristics include: 'Russet' with small leaves and dense foliage on compact branches; 'Samuel Sommer' with extremely fragrant flowers up to 14 inches in diameter and leaves 10 inches or more in length; and 'St. Mary', a small form which grows to 20 feet, is ideal for small garden or street use, and has an especially heavy bloom. 'Edith Bogue' is one of the hardiest cultivars.

Magnolia x soulangiana
Saucer Magnolia
Zones: 5-10. To 20-25 feet.
Deciduous.

This beautiful plant is usually a spreading multistemmed shrub that can be trained as a small tree. Heavy bloom of bold flowers with the outside of the petals lavender-colored and the inside of the petals white appears before leaves unfold. Begins to bloom when it is 3 to 5 years old. Use as a specimen plant on the lawn, small patio tree, or in open woodlands where shade is not too heavy. Prefers full sun but will grow in light shade. 'Superba' has large light purple and white flowers; 'Burgundy' has flowers that are purple halfway up the outside of the petals. The petals of 'Lombardy Rose' are dark rose outside and white inside. There are many other varieties whose flower colors range from dark purple to pure white.

Saucer magnolia (*Magnolia x soulangiana*)

Star magnolia (*Magnolia stellata*)

Magnolia stellata
Star Magnolia
Zones: 5-10. To 8-10 feet.
Deciduous.

Usually a spreading multistemmed shrub, star magnolia can be trained successfully as a small tree. Heavy bloom of fragrant white flowers appears in early spring, before the leaves unfold. Plants bloom when 3 years old. Blossoms are frequently killed by late spring freezes in Zone 5. Use in borders, foundation plantings around large buildings, or at the edge of woodlands. The cultivar 'Royal Star' has large fragrant double flowers, and blooms later than the species.

Malus
Flowering Crab Apple

This genus contains 30 species of deciduous, many-branched trees native to the North Temperate Zone. Both apples and crab apples are included and are distinguished by the size of the fruits. An apple has fruits over 2 inches in diameter, while crab apples have fruits less than 2 inches in diameter.

Crab apples are one of the most ornamental groups of flowering trees. They are grown for their masses of fragrant spring flowers, which range in color from white, pink, red to purplish red. Many have outstanding displays of red, yellow, or orange fruit in late summer or early fall that hang on after leaves drop. Over 600 hybrids, varieties, and cultivars have been named. Often a hundred different types can be found in a nursery. Trees come in a variety of shapes and sizes and fit into many landscape situations.

They vary in height from shrub-like plants such as sargent crab apple, which seldom exceeds 6 to 8 feet, to tall trees like Jack crab apple, which may be 40 feet high. A weeping form is 'White Cascade'. 'Velvet Pillar' is a new upright-growing form.

Types bearing small fruits should be chosen because birds will usually eat the fruit, eliminating the ground litter of larger, uneaten apples. If you wish to grow a dual-purpose crab apple and use the apples for eating, plant one of the large-fruited crab apples, such as

'Centennial'. They have palatable fruit that can be eaten fresh, or made into jelly or applesauce. If you do not wish to have fruiting trees, some cultivars, such as 'Spring Snow', flower abundantly but do not set fruit.

Best growth is made in sandy loam or silty clay soils, but the trees are not choosey and will grow in many soils as long as they are well drained. Do not plant in excessively moist areas. To obtain maximum flowering and fruit set, plant in full sun. Crab apples require average fertility. Excessive fertilization can cause succulent growth that is susceptible to disease.

Some crab apples are quite susceptible to a number of diseases including apple scab and fireblight. Some old time favorites, such as 'Almey', 'Flame', 'Eleyi', and 'Hopa', are so susceptible to disease that more resistant cultivars are replacing them. Apple scab can cause heavy leaf defoliation by midsummer. Fireblight infects trees through wounds, and is carried by insects to the blossoms. In areas where fireblight or apple scab can be a problem, select resistant trees. Fireblight can kill entire branches or even the entire tree. Gypsy moth and tent caterpillar are often severe problems.

Use crab apples as specimen or accent trees in the lawn or garden. Plant fruitless varieties to screen a patio, line a driveway, or for an espalier.

Malus floribunda
Japanese Flowering Crab Apple
Zones: 4-8. To 20-25 feet.
Deciduous.

This is one of the oldest of all known ornamental crab apples and its origin is lost in antiquity. Its shape is broad and rounded with a densely branched crown. Flower buds are deep pink to red, flowers fade to white. Fruits are red-and-yellow, 3/8 inch in diameter, and look showy from August to November. Not completely resistant to fireblight, but has good resistance to scab.

'Red Jade' crab apples *(Malus sp.)* produce a profusion of white flowers on weeping branches in early spring and red fruits in fall.

Flowering crab apples *(Malus sp.)* are excellent plants for lining paths or driveways.

'Radiant' crab apple (Malus sp.)

Flaxleaf paperbark (Melaleuca linariifolia), a top-rated evergreen, bears fluffy white flowers in summer.

Oleanders (Nerium oleander) are excellent flowering evergreen trees for hot summer climates.

Malus
'Radiant'
Zones: 4-8. To 25-30 feet. Deciduous.

A neat compact tree with upright growth. Flower buds are deep red, flowers pink. Bright red fruits, 1/2 inch in diameter, persist into winter. Susceptible to apple scab; resistant to fireblight.

Malus
'Red Jade'
Zones: 4-8. To 15-20 feet. Deciduous.

'Red Jade' has spreading, weeping branches, and bears small white flowers. Tends to bear heavily one year and not the next. Small, red fruits, 1/2 inch in diameter, resemble red jade. Fruit persists into winter or until eaten by birds. Use as a specimen tree. Good disease resistance, but slightly susceptible to scab.

Malus
'Snowdrift'
Zones: 4-8. To 20-25 feet. Deciduous.

Tree with broad oval head. Flower buds are pink, opening to white flowers. Orange-red fruits, 3/8 inch in diameter, persist after leaves drop. Do not plant where fireblight is a severe problem. Resistant to apple scab.

Other crab apples resistant to scab include: 'Adams' with pink flowers and 1/2-inch red fruits; 'White Angel' with white flowers and 3/4-inch red fruits; 'Mary Potter' with white flowers and 1/2-inch red fruits; and 'Sargent' with white flowers and tiny red fruits.

Malus x zumi 'Calocarpa'
Redbud Flowering Crab Apple
Zones: 4-8. To 20-25 feet. Deciduous.

This tree, with a dense, upright growth habit, is completely covered with fragrant blossoms. Deep red flower buds open to white flowers in midspring. Abundant red fruits, 3/8 inch in diameter, persist into winter, or until eaten by birds. Do not plant where fireblight is a severe problem.

Melaleuca
Melaleuca

Native to Australia, these evergreen trees and shrubs are grown for their showy flower clusters and tolerance to drought conditions. New growth develops from tips of flower clusters, resulting in the stems being surrounded by decorative, persistent seed capsules. Trees can be used as specimen or street trees, or as a trimmed hedge.

Melaleuca linariifolia
Flaxleaf Paperbark
Zones: 9-10. To 20-30 feet. Evergreen.

Tree growth is rapid, open, and willowy when young, but becomes umbrella-shaped and dense with age. Bark is white and spongy on young trees, but becomes light brown, papery, and peeling on older limbs and trunks. The stiff, needlelike, bright bluish-green leaves are 1-1/4 inches long. Fluffy white flowers occur in 1- to 2-inch spikes at the ends of the slender branchlets. When in full bloom in summer the tree appears to be covered with snow.

Melaleuca quinquenervia
(M. leucadendra)
Cajeput Tree
Zones: 9-10. To 20-40 feet. Evergreen.

This is a favorite tree for windbreaks and specimen use. Grows rapidly, forming an oval to rounded, open crown and weeping branch tips. Thick, spongy, light brown to whitish bark peels in papery layers. The stiff, narrowly oval, pale green leaves are 2 to 4 inches long and 3/8 to 3/4 inch wide. Yellowish-white, bottlebrush-like flower spikes, 2 to 4 inches long, appear from June to October. Plants with pink or purplish flowers are occasionally seen. Grows best in sun and average soil, but tolerates poor drainage, drought, wind, salt spray, and grass fires. In moist soil areas, seedlings grow readily, quickly becoming problem weeds.

Nerium oleander

Oleander

Zones: 8-10. To 8-20 feet.
Evergreen.

An attractive evergreen, oleander flourishes in hot, dry interior areas and also will grow in coastal locations. It is very adaptable and has one of the longest flowering seasons of any tree.

Oleanders usually develop a broad, bulky form at a moderate to fast rate, and are often used for hedges and screens. A small single- or multiple-trunked tree, with branches starting at 7 or 8 feet, can be developed by pruning. 'Sister Agnes', which has single white flowers, grows to 20 feet, and would be a good choice for use as a tree.

Thick, glossy dark green leaves 3 to 6 inches long and 3/4 to 1 inch wide are usually in whorls of three. Forms with leaves to 12 inches long, and golden-variegated leaves are sometimes available. Brilliant, waxy flowers from 1-1/2 to 3 inches wide are borne in clusters at twig or branch tips from May or June to September. Varieties with single or double flowers in white, yellow, salmon, pink, and red are available. Some varieties have fragrant blooms.

Oleanders are not particular about soil and withstand considerable drought, poor drainage, and relatively high salt levels. They also take heat and strong light, including reflected heat from paving, and tolerate wind, air pollution, and salt spray.

Growth is best in full sun in moist, well-drained soil. In shade or in cool locations, few flowers develop and growth is weak and leggy. Water infrequently in late summer and fall so growth hardens before cold weather begins. Prune in early spring to control size and form. Cut off stem tips that have flowered to increase branching. Pull, don't cut, suckers, which occur at the base of the plant, to prevent bushiness.

Pest problems of oleander include yellow oleander aphid, scale insects, and bacterial gall. One spray

Oleanders *(Nerium oleander)* give an extended summer bloom when few other trees are in flower.

Cajeput tree *(Melaleuca quinquenervia)*

Sourwoods *(Oxydendrum arboreum)* produce long sprays of white, bell-shaped flowers in summer.

'Krauter Vesuvius' *(Prunus cerasifera)* is one of the smallest purple-leaf plums. Blossom shown below.

in the spring usually controls aphids. Bacterial gall causes deformed flowers and warty, split stems. It is best controlled by pruning diseased branches well below the infected area.

All parts of oleander are poisonous to people and livestock. Don't use the wood for barbeque skewers. Also, smoke from burning plant parts can cause severe irritation.

Oxydendrum arboreum
Sourwood, Sorrel Tree

Zones: 6-9. To 15-25 feet. Deciduous.

A choice narrow, pyramidal tree, sourwood is planted for creamy white bell-shaped flowers that hang in drooping, 10-inch-long clusters in midsummer. Ornamental brown seed pods follow flowering. Rich green summer foliage turns to orange and red in fall. Tree grows slowly to 25 feet; may eventually reach 50 feet. Growth is best in cool summer areas of Zones 6 to 8. Needs moist, acid, well-drained soil, and full sun.

Parkinsonia aculeata
Jerusalem Thorn

Zones: 8-10. To 25-30 feet. Deciduous.

Jerusalem thorn is most valuable in the arid Southwest where it provides light shade and yellow flowers in areas where few other trees will grow. Leaves are divided into many tiny leaflets and arranged sparsely on the greenish-yellow, thorned branches. They drop quickly during drought or cold. Withstands alkaline soil, heat, and drought.

Prunus
Flowering Fruit, Prunus

Many beautiful and useful ornamental trees and shrubs are found in this large genus. Many of the most popular tree fruits, such as almond, apricot, cherry, nectarine,

peach, plum, and prune, are included. Selections have been made in all these groups for forms with superior flowers, but flowering cherries and plums are the most widely planted.

Evergreen species of *Prunus* are often used for screens, clipped hedges, and specimen trees. Deciduous types require a winter cold period for the flowers and leaves to develop normally. All grow best in well-drained soils.

Prunus x blireiana
Blireiana Plum
Zones: 5-9. To 20-25 feet. Deciduous.

This hybrid of *P. cerasifera* 'Atropurpurea' and *P. mume* has the purple leaves of the plum and the semidouble, fragrant flowers of the Japanese apricot. The tree is dense and rounded with slender branches. The reddish-purple leaves turn greenish bronze in summer. Pink, 1-inch flowers are borne on bare branches in late winter to early spring. Fruits are the same color as the leaves but few are produced. Pruning and thinning are needed to reduce the wind resistance of these shallow-rooted plants and to encourage a tree shape. Young trees should be staked.

Prunus caroliniana
Carolina Cherry Laurel
Zones: 7-10. To 20-40 feet. Evergreen.

A large shrub or small tree, this species is top-rated as a large screen or clipped hedge. It can also be trained as a dense, broad-topped, single- or multiple-trunked tree. It is adapted to warm climates such as its native North Carolina to Texas region. Small, cream-white flowers in 1-inch spikes open between February and April. Black fruits, 1/2 inch or less in diameter, tend to persist if the birds don't eat them. Falling fruits and flowers can be messy on paved areas. Growth rate is moderate to rapid. Leaves are medium to dark, glossy green, 2 to 4 inches long, and have smooth edges. New growth is bronze-colored.

Carolina cherry laurel grows well in average soil, but may show salt burn and chlorosis in alkaline soil. Although growth is best in coastal areas, it can take full sun and high heat. Pruning is needed to achieve the desired tree shape. Problems include scale insects and the disease fireblight.

Prunus cerasifera 'Atropurpurea'
Purple-Leaf Plum
Zones: 5-9. To 15-30 feet.
Deciduous.

Purple-leaf plums are one of the trees most asked for in garden centers. Their beautiful foliage provides a color accent from spring to fall, extending the short period most flowering trees are colorful. This variety was the first of the type to become popular, and is often called 'Pissardii' for the French gardener who found it growing in Iran.

The vase shape of young trees changes into a very dense, rounded shape with age. The spring foliage is coppery-red when the flowers are opening, changing to dark wine-red. The 1-1/2 to 2-1/2-inch-long leaves fade to greenish bronze in the summer, and drop without a color change. Masses of white to pink, single, fragrant flowers, 3/4 to 1 inch in diameter, open in early spring, but do not last long. Heavy crops of small, edible red or yellow plums, 1 inch in diameter, often develop. This fruit can be messy if it drops on a paved area.

Purple-leaf plum should be grown in full sun and a well-drained soil. Subject to limb breakage from ice, wet snow, and wind. Prune to remove crossing limbs. Does not grow well in polluted air.

Other top-rated purple-leaf plums are:

'Hollywood': This is a hybrid between *P. cerasifera* 'Atropurpurea' and 'Duarte' plum. It is adapted to Zones 5 to 9. Becomes 30 to 40 feet tall and 25 feet wide. Bluntly oval leaves are green in the spring, but undersides are deep red. Whitish-pink flowers in early spring are followed by tasty, 2-inch fruit in early summer.

'Shirotae' Japanese flowering cherry *(Prunus serrulata)*

'Shirotae' Japanese flowering cherries *(Prunus serrulata)* are wide-spreading trees covered with a mass of blooms in spring.

'Kwanzan' (*Prunus serrulata*) is the hardiest, most widely used Japanese flowering cherry.

'Kwanzan' Japanese cherry (*Prunus sp.*)

'Krauter Vesuvius': Sometimes called 'Vesuvius' this is one of the smaller-growing purple-leaf plums. Expect a height of 18 feet and a width of 12 feet. Leaves are larger and darker purple than the other selections, but tree does not produce as heavy a bloom. Flowers are light pink.

'Thundercloud': Top-rated because the deep coppery-purple leaves hold their color throughout the growing season. Grows to 25 feet with a round, ball shape. Light pink to white flowers come out before the leaves.

Prunus x cistena
Purple-Leaf Sand Cherry
Zones: 3-9. To 8-10 feet.
Deciduous.

Hybridized in the early 1900's by Dr. N. E. Hansen of the South Dakota State Experiment Station by crossing *P. besseyi* with *P. cerasifera* 'Atropurpurea', this is usually a multibranched shrub used as a screen or clipped hedge. Purple-leaf sand cherry can be trained as a handsome, single-trunk tree. Excellent as a color-accent tree in small areas.

Young crimson leaves are 1-1/2 to 2-1/2 inches long, and remain bronze-red all summer. White to pinkish flowers open in early spring just before the tree leafs out. Blackish-purple fruit ripens in July. Grow in full sun and well-drained soil.

Prunus serrulata
Japanese Flowering Cherry
Zones: 6-9. To 20-25 feet.
Deciduous.

One of the showiest spring-flowering trees, this flowering cherry is native to Japan and China. As the national tree of Japan, it is planted on the grounds of temples, shrines and parks. Other plants grow well under its branches, making it a gardener's favorite. Flowers can be single or double, white or pink, and range from 1/2 to 2-1/2 inches in diameter. Has beautiful shiny bark.

Use as a specimen, or street tree, or in masses. In the eastern United States, Zone 8 is the southern limit for good growth.

All flowering cherries should be grown in full sun. They are somewhat drought-tolerant but grow better with summer irrigation. A well-drained soil is preferred but with care trees can succeed in clay soils. Cherry slugs and tent caterpillars are pests. Small branches are sometimes killed by cherry dead-bud disease.

One hundred or more varieties have been named but top-rated are:

'Amanogawa': A narrow columnar tree, its young yellowish foliage becomes medium green in the summer, and yellow and red in fall. Fragrant light pink semidouble flowers are 1-3/4 inches wide and open early midseason, before or with the leaves.

'Kwanzan': One of the hardiest and most adaptable of the Oriental cherries. 'Sekiyama' is another name for this tree. 'Kwanzan' is the cherry used at the famous tidal basin planting in Washington D.C. New leaves are reddish copper and turn yellow and red in fall. Deep pink, double (30 petals), 2-1/2 inch flowers come out before or with the leaves at midseason. Grows 35 feet tall and wide.

'Shirofugen': Also called 'White Goddess', this is a vigorous, spreading, flat-topped tree that can reach 40 feet wide. Flowers are double (30 petals), 2-1/2 inches wide and change from pink buds to white flowers, finally fading to pale pink with age. Blooms in late spring. Leaves are deep crimson-bronze when young. They are almost full grown and in full color when the flowers open.

'Shirotae' (Mt. Fuji): This is a small, spreading, flat-topped tree that grows 30 feet wide. Young leaves are pale green with a fringed look, later becoming dark green. The white, semidouble flowers are fragrant, 2 to 2-1/2 inches across and open early. A top choice for a white flowering Oriental cherry.

'Ukon': Grown for the unusual semidouble, greenish-yellow flowers opening in early midseason, this tree is sparsely branched, but grows vigorously to 30 feet tall and about as wide. Flowers harmonize nicely with the bronze-colored young foliage. Fall color is orange-red. Branch tips should be pinched on young plants to induce denser growth. Prune as little as possible, only removing crossing limbs.

Prunus subhirtella
Higan Cherry, Weeping Cherry
Zones: 6-9. To 20-30 feet.
Deciduous.

Native to Japan, Korea, and China, this tree flowers before leaves emerge. Small blossoms in 2- to 5-inch clusters appear on short stalks and make a beautiful impact in early spring. Growth is loose with a rounded or flattened outline. Leaves are 1 to 1-2/3 inches long and half as wide.

'Autumnalis': Grown for its double, white or pink flowers that open in autumn and often again in early spring. Reaches 25 feet with an equal or greater spread.

'Pendula': During the midspring flowering season the weeping branches are covered with small pale pink single flowers. Usually grafted high so there is room for drooping branchlets. Main branches arch up and outward, while branchlets are pendulous. Picturesque tree even in off-season. Grows slowly to 10 to 12 feet.

'Yae-Shidare-Higan': Long-lasting, double pink flowers distinguish this weeping cherry variety, sometimes called 'Pendula Plena Rosea'. Grafted high on a 5 to 6 foot rootstock, branches arch upward forming a 12-foot-tall, umbrella-shaped tree with long weeping branchlets. Width of the tree usually equals the height.

Flowering fruit trees *(Prunus sp.)* offer a wide range of blossom color.
Weeping cherry *(Prunus subhirtella)* has dramatic impact in the landscape.

Bradford callery pears *(Pyrus calleryana)* have a formal, oval shape.

Bradford callery pear *(Pyrus calleryana)*

Evergreen pear *(Pyrus kawakamii)*

Pyrus
Pear

There are 20 species of deciduous or semievergreen, small to medium-sized trees in this genus. They originated in Europe, Asia, and North Africa. Most pears that have been selected for cultivation are grown for their fruit and have heavy displays of flowers in the spring. The few selected as ornamentals usually have small inconspicuous fruits.

One of the pests most damaging to pears is fireblight. It can destroy sections of a tree, or even the entire tree. A few ornamentals, such as the callery pear, are resistant to fireblight. Callery pear has been used in breeding work to develop pears with resistance to fireblight. In areas where this disease is a problem, fireblight-resistant pears should be selected.

Pyrus calleryana 'Bradford'
Bradford Callery Pear
Zones: 5-9. To 40-50 feet.
Deciduous.

This is a popular flowering tree in the eastern United States. It has a conical crown when young that becomes rounded or oval as the tree ages. It is covered with masses of white flowers in the spring and glossy dark green leaves in summer. One of the last trees to color in fall, Bradford pear becomes yellow to bronzy-red or purple, and the leaves often hang for two weeks or longer before falling. Russet-brown fruits are 1/2 inch or less, and inconspicuous.

This tough tree will tolerate city pollution. Can be used as a street tree, lawn tree, and specimen or patio tree. Often grown on islands in parking lots. Adaptable to many different soils, but should be planted in full sun. Unlike the species, it is thornless.

Other cultivars of Callery pear are 'Aristocrat' with dark green leaves with wavy edges and 'Faureri', dwarf Korean callery pear, a small tree to 25 feet that is good on windy, exposed sites where breakage would occur on larger trees.

Pyrus kawakamii
Evergreen Pear
Zones: 9-10. To 30 feet.
Evergreen to partially deciduous.

Normally a spreading shrub, evergreen pear is easily trained into a small tree. Glossy, light green leaves are a year-round feature in most areas. Fragrant masses of white flowers in spring. Use as a patio or park tree, or grow in containers. Full sun or light shade and average moisture are required for good growth. A popular plant in California. Evergreen in warm areas, becoming partially deciduous in cold climates.

Robinia
Locust

Locusts are top-rated where a fast-growing, tough, deciduous tree is needed for immediate effect. Brittle wood and invasive roots rule them out in most other situations.

Robinia x ambigua 'Idahoensis'
Idaho Locust
Zones: 5-10. To 40 feet.
Deciduous.

This is the most handsome form of locust. Divided leaves combine to make a tight, compact head. Rosy-pink, pealike blossoms are borne in long clusters from midspring to early summer. Takes drought, poor soils, and high temperatures.

Robinia pseudoacacia
Black Locust
Zones: 3-9. To 60-75 feet.
Deciduous.

Black locust has showy clusters of white fragrant flowers, and interesting furrowed bark. Leaves are divided, and dark green. Thorny branches are covered with 4-inch, beanlike pods in winter. Withstands the same tough conditions as the Idaho locust.

Sophora japonica
Japanese Pagoda Tree, Chinese Scholar Tree

Zones: 5-8. To 30-60 feet.
Deciduous.

Valued for its late-summer flowers, Japanese pagoda tree is tolerant of heat, dryness, and city pollution. For over 1,000 years, this tree has been planted on the grounds of temples in China, Korea, and Japan. It is also top-rated as a shade and flowering tree for American gardens.

Generally a roundheaded tree, as wide as tall, with a short trunk, the tree's growth rate is moderate up to 30 feet, and slow thereafter. Twigs and young branches are smooth and green, while older branches have a pale gray-brown bark. The fernlike, compound leaves are 6 to 10 inches long with 7 to 17 oval, dark green leaflets up to 2 inches long. Leaves drop without changing color in late fall. In late July and August, yellow-white, 1/2-inch, pea-shaped flowers in 8- to 15-inch pyramidal clusters cover the tree. Fallen flowers may stain cement. Pendulous, translucent, 3-inch green pods follow.

Grows best in full sun and well-drained soil. Because of the low branching habit, it is not suitable as a street tree, but it grows well in cities and will tolerate drought and high temperatures. Flowering may be inconsistent in cool, cloudy summer areas. First bloom may take 10 years, but 'Regent' blooms sooner, is more erect, and faster growing.

Sorbus aucuparia
European Mountain Ash

Zones: 2-7. To 45 feet.
Deciduous.

Erect when young, becoming spreading and open at maturity, European mountain ash is frequently a multistemmed tree. Small

Japanese pagoda trees *(Sophora japonica)* are summer-flowering trees noted for their durability in difficult locations.

Black locust *(Robinia pseudoacacia)*

49

European mountain ash trees *(Sorbus aucuparia)* grow tall and usually form multiple-trunks.

European mountain ash *(Sorbus aucuparia):* berries above, blossom below.

white flowers grow in clusters 3 to 5 inches in diameter. Large clusters of bright red to orange-red berries follow in late summer or early fall. Fruit remains until eaten by birds. Compound, pale dull-green leaves turn yellow to red in fall.

The European mountain ash is the principal species used in the United States. It has been planted since Colonial times, and has become naturalized in some areas of North America, including Alaska. Although it will grow on dry sites, best growth is made on rich, moist soils with a pH of 6.0 to 7.5. Will grow in full sun or partial shade. Does not thrive in areas where there is extreme summer heat. Needs to be watered in summer.

Use as a specimen or lawn tree, also as a street tree on the Pacific Coast. Not a tree to be planted and neglected, it is subject to borers at the base of tree, which may require sprays to control. In areas where Japanese beetles are a problem, the leaves may have to be sprayed with an insecticide to keep the adult beetles from destroying the foliage. Fireblight also can be a problem in some areas.

A number of cultivars and hybrids have been developed. 'Brilliant Yellow' has golden yellow fruit. 'Cardinal Royal' has large clusters of bright red berries, coloring earlier than the species. 'Charming Pink' has pink fruit. 'Fastigiata' has a columnar shape. The hybrid 'Meinichii' has a pyramidal shape with larger berries than the species and larger green leaves.

The genus *Sorbus* is comprised of many ornamental trees and shrubs in addition to the European mountain ash. Several of these are excellent landscape plants but are not considered top-rated because they are not widely available in nurseries. *S. alnifolia,* Korean mountain ash, is particularly noteworthy.

The Korean mountain ash grows 25 to 35 feet tall and, unlike most other members of this genus, has simple undivided leaves and is resistant to borer attack. The foliage is a deep lustrous green and turns crimson and scarlet in fall. Small

clusters of snow-white flowers are borne in spring. They are followed by bright red berries. The tree's silvery-gray bark is attractive in winter. Korean mountain ash is adapted to Zones 4 to 8.

Stewartia pseudocamellia

Japanese Stewartia

Zones: 6-9. To 30-60 feet. Deciduous.

An unusual and rarely grown tree, Japanese stewartia has white, single, camellia-type flowers in the summer, yellow, red, or purple fall color, and striking, flaking bark. Slow-growing, trees need moist, but well-drained, acid soil. Suitable for all but the hottest parts of Zones 6 to 9.

Styrax japonicus

Japanese Snowbell

Zones: 6-9. To 30 feet. Deciduous.

Pendulous, white bell-shaped flowers line the undersides of the horizontal branches in late spring or early summer, while leaves angle upwards. Forms a flat-topped tree with attractive bark. Needs partial shade or full sun and acid, well-drained soil with ample organic matter. Use as a specimen or lawn tree, next to patios, or in wooded areas.

Wisteria

Wisteria

Beautiful, long drooping flower clusters are the major feature of wisterias. Normally wisterias are vigorous vines useful for shade, screening, and decorative effects, but with pruning and training, a small, flowering tree with a weeping shape can be developed.

Choose a grafted plant or one grown from a cutting, since they bloom earlier than a seedling. It is sometimes possible to buy a wisteria trained as a tree, or you can train your own. Select a single stem and tie it with plastic tape at frequent intervals to a pipe stake. When the stem grows to the desired height for the head, remove the stem tip to induce branching. A multistemmed tree can also be grown in the same way. Keep branches shortened, so they become thicker. Pinch any long shoots that form and rub off any buds that appear on the trunk below the head. Replace or loosen ties periodically so growth is not strangled.

Wisterias should be grown in full sun in a good loam soil for best results. Fertilize young plants. Water blooming plants for best flowering. Pruning should be done each winter: remove excess branches and shorten flower-producing spurs to 2 or 3 large flower buds.

Wisteria floribunda
Japanese Wisteria
Zones: 5-9.
Deciduous.

Dark green divided leaves, 12 to 16 inches long, have 13 to 19 leaflets. Stems twist clockwise as they climb, while those of the Chinese wisteria twist counterclockwise. Fragrant, violet-blue flowers open in succession from the base to the tip of the 10- to 18-inch clusters. Flowers open as the leaves start to develop. The blooming period is longer, but the color impact less, than with the Chinese wisteria. Many varieties with white, pink, blue, purple, or lavender flowers are available.

Wisteria sinensis
Chinese Wisteria
Zones: 5-9.
Deciduous.

Chinese wisteria leaves are divided into 9 to 13 leaflets. Has 1-inch-long, slightly fragrant, violet-blue flowers, larger than those of the Japanese wisteria. All flowers on the 6- to 12-inch clusters open at one time making a spectacular show. Blooms before the leaves expand in April to May.

Wisterias *(Wisteria sp.)* trained as small trees bear long clusters of intensely fragrant spring flowers.

Japanese wisteria *(Wisteria floribunda)*

Caring for Flowering Trees

Flowering trees are an investment. You'll receive full value from them by keeping the trees you have selected in good condition until planted, and planting with care. Proper soil preparation and planting technique are important, as is regular watering until the tree is established.

Home from the Nursery

Nurseries offer flowering trees in three forms: bareroot, balled-and-burlapped, and in containers.

Bareroot: These are field-grown, deciduous trees that are dug up while dormant and handled with little or no soil on the roots, hence the term "bareroot". They should be planted as early in the growing season as possible, soon after the danger of soil freezing has passed. Look for trees with good-sized, well-balanced roots. Lateral roots should radiate from the main roots in several directions on several levels. Leaf and flower buds should be plump and firm, not dried up.

If you cannot plant the tree right away, pack its roots in moist peat moss, sawdust, or soil. Keep it in the shade with the roots as cool as possible without freezing.

Balled-and-burlapped: These trees are field-grown, then dug, and the ball of roots and soil is wrapped for shipping. They can be planted year-round, though spring and fall are preferred. When handling balled-and-burlapped trees be careful to lift them from the bottom. Do not use the trunk as a handle. Before planting keep them from falling over by lightly securing the trunk to a fence or wedging the ball between other heavy objects.

Close observation of plants helps detect any problems early for prompt treatment.

Chinese fringe tree (*Chionanthus sp.*)

Lemon bottlebrush (*Callistemon sp.*)

Keep the foliage moist if the tree has leafed-out (leaves have appeared), and water the rootball frequently and slowly from the top. Keep the tree shaded and out of the wind until planting.

Container: Many nursery plants are container-grown. Available throughout the growing season, they are convenient for the home gardener since they don't have to be planted right away.

Containers are usually plastic or metal. Most nursery personnel will offer to cut the sides of metal cans for you. This makes planting easier, but is recommended *only if you plan to plant the same day.* Once cans are cut the rootball dries out quickly.

Many containers are made of dark-colored materials, which heat rapidly when exposed to full sun. Shade the container with a board, mounded soil, or low wall.

Soil

Proper amounts of water, air, and nutrients are essential for root growth. Soil composition determines how much of these is available for a plant's use, so check your soil type before planting.

Clay soils are composed of small mineral particles that cling tightly to moisture and nutrients, leaving little room for air. A handful of heavy clay soil feels sticky and squeezes through your fingers in ribbons. Overwatering heavy clay soils is a potential problem. Though the surface appears dry, the root area may be saturated with water—and constant saturation and poor aeration can damage roots.

Sandy soils are composed of relatively large mineral particles. Water and nutrients pass through sandy soils quickly. A handful of moist, sandy soil squeezed into a ball crumbles when released. There is plenty of air for root growth but frequent watering is necessary. Fertilizers must be applied more lightly and frequently.

Loam soils are intermediate between clay and sandy soils, combining the best characteristics of each. Loam soils retain moisture and nutrients but still allow for good aeration and drainage. A handful of squeezed loam soil forms a loosely packed ball.

SOIL pH

Chemists measure soil acidity and alkalinity on the pH scale. It ranges from 0 to 14, with the low numbers indicating acidity and the high numbers alkalinity. Midpoint, 7, is neutral.

Soil pH may vary from garden to garden but generally is determined by the amount of rainfall an area receives. Rain washes natural limestone from soil, increasing its acidity. Areas of high rainfall have the most acid soil; areas of low rainfall have alkaline soil.

You can measure the pH of your garden soil by using one of the simple test kits available at most garden centers. Or, ask your local county agricultural extension office about university or private laboratory soil tests.

DRAINAGE

The rate of water drainage where you are planting is important. While most flowering trees adapt to many different soils, few flourish where drainage is slow. If drainage is too slow, air is forced from the soil and roots drown.

Check drainage before planting by filling a hole with water and letting it drain. Refill the hole with water and time how long it takes to drain. Water should drain at least one-quarter inch per hour. Most soil drains much faster, but if yours does not, you have two choices: Plant in raised beds or mounds, or bore through the impervious soil with a post-hole digger until the water drains at an acceptable rate. Then fill the bored hole with soil that has been amended to drain faster.

Planting

In most areas, fall is the best time to plant. Temperatures are moderate then and soil is relatively warm, encouraging root growth. If you live where soil might freeze, plant in early fall and mulch after planting. The mulch will moderate temperatures, preventing the alternate freezing and thawing that damages roots of partially established plants.

Spring is the recommended planting time where winters are regularly severe. Again, temperatures are moderate, minimizing stress on plants.

Summer planting is usually not recommended. High heat, coupled with limited roots, is often enough to kill young plants. However, if you shade plants and give extra attention to watering, summer planting can be successful. In many areas, winter planting is prevented by snow cover or frozen soil. Where soil remains workable, winter planting is successful if necessary wind protection is provided.

THE PLANTING HOLE

Planting techniques vary depending upon whether you are planting a bareroot, balled-and-burlapped, or a container-grown tree. But for all three types, you should start with a hole that is twice the width of the roots and six inches deeper. If the soil you dug out of the hole is very sandy or heavy clay, mix two parts soil with organic material such as compost, peat moss, or shredded bark. Use this amended soil as backfill to refill the hole around and under the tree's roots. If you are planting from containers, this 2-to-1 mix provides a transition between the usually lightweight container soil mix and heavier garden soil.

Soak and firm amended soil in the bottom of planting hole to prevent excessive settling.

Do not mix fertilizer in the hole or with backfill soil. Young roots can be damaged by direct contact with fertilizer. Sprinkle fertilizer on top of the soil and around the plant, then water in.

HOW TO PLANT

Bareroot planting: Check the roots carefully, cutting back any that are broken. If the roots appear to be dried or withered, soak them in water overnight. Form a cone of soil in the center of the planting hole. Spread the roots over the cone, then add amended soil to the hole gradually, firming it as you go. When the hole is about three-quarters full, soak the soil with water. Finish filling the hole, pack the soil, then form a watering basin (low ridge around the edge of the filled hole) to hold water.

Balled-and-burlapped planting: Be careful when moving a balled-and-burlapped tree. Use both hands under the rootball or, if the tree is very heavy, get someone to help you carry it on a tarp or a piece of canvas. Set the rootball on a mound of backfill soil in the planting hole. The plant should sit 1 or 2 inches higher than nursery soil level to allow for soil settling. Add soil to cover the bottom third of the rootball, cut the twine, and lay back the

Soil

Clay soil has smooth texture and retains moisture.

Sandy soil is gritty, loose, and fast-draining.

Loam soil combines the best features of clay and sandy soils.

Planting

1. Mix organic amendment into garden soil to make backfill mix.

2. Add backfill to planting hole to a depth of about 8 inches.

3. Add water to planting hole to moisten and settle backfill.

4. Loosen roots that the container has forced to coil or circle, and set rootball in planting hole.

5. Add backfill around rootball, firming with your hands as you go.

6. Be sure the original rootball receives ample water the first year after planting.

burlap. Do not remove the burlap; it will eventually rot away. Add more soil, firming it as you do.

Some tree rootballs need support if there is any possibility of the plant falling over after planting. Drive three short stakes into solid ground, attaching them with rope to the trunk 6 to 12 inches above soil level.

Many larger balled-and-burlapped and container-grown trees will need 1 or 2 tall stakes for trunk support. Drive stakes as close as possible to the rootball. Strips of cloth, plastic tree tape, or twine enclosed by a section of garden hose all serve well to attach the trunk to the stakes.

A tree will become stronger and support itself sooner if allowed to sway somewhat with the wind. Attach trunk support stakes no higher than necessary and remove stakes as soon as possible. Be sure to check ties often to ensure they do not damage the bark of the tree trunk.

Once the hole is filled and packed and the tree is staked, form a water basin surrounding the original rootball, then flood it several times to soak rootball and soil thoroughly.

Container-grown planting: The planting process for container plants is essentially the same as that used with balled-and-burlapped plants. However, the roots of container plants might need extra attention. Once you have removed the can, examine the roots. If they're crowded or coiled on the surface, loosen them with a stick or knife and head them away from the trunk. Cut off any badly damaged roots.

Watering

Keeping a newly planted tree moist during its first growing season is essential to its continued well-being. There are a number of ways to water efficiently: basins, furrows (these are trenches running parallel on either side of trees), sprinklers, soaker hoses, and drip systems—all will get water to plants. The goal is to eliminate run-off, apply water uniformly, and confine water to inside the tree's drip line (an imaginary area on the ground beneath the outer leaves of a plant). By far the most efficient method of achieving all these, especially when you're trying to establish new plants, is some form of drip irrigation.

Mulching

Mulching is an effective way to conserve moisture. A mulch is an insulating layer applied on top of soil to cover and protect it. Mulches are organic, such as compost, sawdust, bark, wood chips, or straw; or inorganic, such as plastic or stone. Mulches cool soil, an important consideration during hot summers, help prevent weeds and soil compaction and give a finished appearance to a planting. Organic mulches improve soil texture.

Fertilizing

Nitrogen is the only element most trees require from a fertilizer. Young trees may grow more rapidly following nitrogen fertilization, but mature trees usually need little or no fertilization as long as they have good leaf color and are growing well.

Let the tree's condition be your guide to fertilizing. Needlessly stimulating growth may result in more harm than good. Soft, oversized leaves forced by overfertilization are more attractive to insect and disease pests and consume more water.

Flowering trees deficient in nitrogen have light yellow foliage and grow slowly. The yellowing is most evident on older leaves. Fertilize in late fall or while dormant. Fertilize trees in sandy soil 2 or 3 weeks before spring growth to minimize loss of fertilizer by leaching rainfall. Applications in late summer or early fall stimulate growth that may be harmed by fall frosts.

Fertilizer recommendations are usually made in pounds of actual nitrogen. To determine how much actual nitrogen is in a fertilizer, divide the amount of nitrogen you need by the first number of the fertilizer analysis on the bag (the first number is always the number for nitrogen). For example, if you want 1 pound of actual nitrogen and your fertilizer analysis is 20-0-0, divide 1 by 20 percent (.20). You will need 5 pounds of 20-0-0 to equal 1 pound of actual nitrogen.

Infertile soils may require annual applications of about 1 to 1-1/2 pounds of nitrogen per mature tree each year. New plants that show need of nitrogen are adequately served by applying 3 to 6 ounces of actual nitrogen per 100 square feet. Keep fertilizer away from the trunk and apply in a circle 1-1/4 times the radius of the tree's canopy.

Pruning

Flowering trees are pruned for many reasons. Pruning right after planting compensates for root loss on bareroot trees and improves water balance (ratio of root area to leaf area) of container-grown trees. Both young and mature trees are pruned to remove deadwood and crossed branches, and to allow more light and air into the tree's interior.

Pruning is particularly useful in controlling tree size. Even significantly overgrown flowering trees can be brought down to appropriate size without damaging their structure or appearance.

PRUNING YOUNG TREES

The first 2 to 3 years after planting are the most important in developing the permanent framework of a young tree. Before pruning a newly planted tree, consider again how you're going to use it in your landscape and its particular growth habits. The height of the first permanent branch depends on what you want the tree to do. Is it going to screen an unwanted view? Does there need to be room for children to play beneath it? The position of a branch on the trunk remains the same throughout the life of a tree. As it increases in diameter, the branch gets somewhat closer to the ground.

As you examine your young tree, identify the leader, or main stem, which will be the trunk of the tree. Unless it is a multistemmed type, remove any competing leaders.

Watering

Drip watering systems are efficient. They apply water directly over roots at a rate soil can absorb.

A basin of firmed soil directs water to roots—however periodic repair is required.

Trees planted in lawns need occasional deep watering in addition to normal lawn sprinkling.

Mulching

Bark mulch is available in many sizes. Use uniform-size particles to give plantings a neat appearance.

Rock mulch does not wash away and lasts indefinitely, but does not add humus to soil.

Irregular particles of low-cost shredded bark bind together to form a mulch that will hold well on slopes.

Fertilizing

Spray leaves with foliar fertilizer for fastest results.

Subsurface injector delivers water and nutrients directly to root zone.

Granular fertilizer applied on surface can promote good tree growth but often is consumed primarily by lawn.

Now select two to four scaffold (primary) branches that will give you the amount of room you want beneath the tree. You may have to wait for a season or two of growth before you can chose scaffold branches at the right height.

Try to choose scaffold branches that are at a wide, 60° to 90°, angle to the trunk. This angle will give a tree a full shape and allow strong branches to develop. Cut the scaffold branches back to an outward-facing bud so they grow away from the trunk.

Cut back any branches below this height to a single bud. A small amount of foliage along the main trunk will help strengthen it and prevents sunburn. Continue to keep these short lateral branches pruned back so small bunches of foliage are retained. Remove these completely when the tree matures.

The second year's pruning is often critical in the life of a young tree. A well-cared-for young tree is likely to produce heavier shoots and foliage than the leader can support and some branches may even break off. Prune to remove this weight, keeping in mind the kind of tree shape you want to encourage. For an open tree leave the terminal (end) shoot on the scaffold branches and shorten or remove all side shoots. For a compact shape, cut the terminals back to a side shoot on each branch. This will help the branches grow thicker and more horizontally.

PRUNING SPRING-FLOWERING TREES

Most trees that flower in spring do so on buds of one-year-old wood—the growth of the previous summer. Prune these trees at the end of their bloom period in late spring. If pruned in late summer, fall, or winter, many flower buds are lost.

Several spring-flowering trees produce showy fruit in the summer or fall. In these cases, compromise between maximum spring flower display and maximum fruit development. Crab apples, for instance, are usually pruned in winter.

PRUNING SUMMER-FLOWERING TREES

Trees in this category usually produce flowers on new spring growth. If you prune in spring after growth begins, you may cut off potential flower buds. Prune these trees in late winter or early spring before new growth begins.

PRUNING MATURE TREES

Prune full-size trees by removing dead or interfering branches. Follow the suggestions below for maintaining size and proper density.

Thinning: Thinning is necessary when the interior growth of a tree becomes too dense and casts too heavy a shade. When a tree is thinned, branches—large or small—are removed at their points of origin or cut back to other branches. Thinning gives a tree a more open structure. After thinning, the new growth follows the tree's natural branching pattern and tends to be evenly distributed throughout the crown. Any crossed branches should be removed while still small.

Heading back: Heading back is done to encourage denser, more compact growth, but results in less strongly attached branches which are more likely to break. Hedges and screens are commonly headed back. To head back a tree, cut off the end of a limb or branch to a lateral bud, or a small lateral branch.

Bareroot trees are both top- and root-pruned at the nursery. They are also commonly headed at planting time. Very upright growing trees can be headed low, within 3 feet of the ground. Trees with a weeping growth habit require high heading, about 6 feet from the ground. Most trees are headed at 4 to 5 feet from soil level. Low heading stimulates many new shoots, but some may be too low to use. High-headed trees are more likely to require staking.

Shearing is a method of heading back that is used to make tailored hedges. Use long-handled hedge shears or electric hedge shears to cut across many leaves and small branches at once.

When mature trees are headed it is called "stubbing". Resulting growth is twiggy and rarely attractive.

Problems and Solutions

Some flowering trees are prone to attack by insect pests such as aphids, scale, borers, and caterpillars. Fireblight and scab are two diseases that can infect some species of flowering trees. General information on specific pests and diseases is included in the encyclopedia section where appropriate. You will also find a column in the care charts on pages 60 to 62 that tells you whether or not a flowering tree is considered pest-resistant. Using this information as a guide when selecting plants can help keep your garden more problem-free.

Insect pests and diseases can be controlled chemically, physically, or biologically. The tendency in recent years has been away from chemical spraying in favor of physical controls—such as hosing pests off—and biological controls—encouraging useful insects such as ladybugs and lacewings to stay in the garden.

It is beyond the scope of this book to recommend a specific treatment program for every potential insect pest or disease. Effective control techniques vary in different growing regions and can depend on other variable factors such as season and type of weather when treatment is administered.

If you spot symptoms of pests or diseases, such as sudden wilting of flowering shoots, darkened or spotted leaves, dead branches, or unusual sloughing of trunk bark, cut off a small portion of the infected plant, and take the cutting to your garden center. Your nurseryman can usually identify the problem and suggest treatment.

Problems can be minimized by following good maintenance procedures in your garden and being observant. Early detection of insect pests or diseases and promptly taking control measures can help keep problems from becoming serious.

Pruning

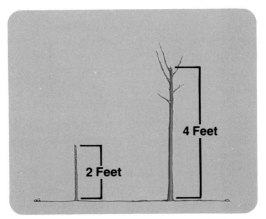

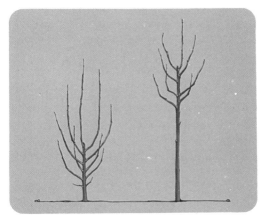

Bareroot tree at planting: (left) If poorly branched, cut off all limbs forcing new growth; (right) If well-branched, thin and head back 1/2 of growth.

Heading bareroot tree at planting: (left) Low heading; (right) High heading.

Headed trees after 1 year: (left) Low heading forces new shoots, some low; (right) High-headed trees tend to lean in wind and trunks may sun-scald.

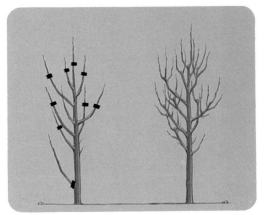

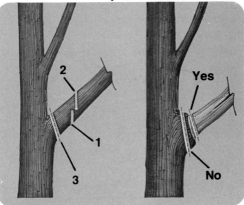

Thin to reduce development of new shoots and direct growth: (left) Thinning cuts made; (right) Resulting growth.

Head to increase the number of new shoots and stiffen branches: (left) Heading cuts made; (right) Resulting growth.

To remove heavy limb (left): 1) under-cut, 2) cut through limb, 3) remove stub. To remove dead stub (right): Cut flush with healthy growth, not trunk.

Problems and Solutions

Take advantage of the gardening expertise available at your local garden center.

Aphids are common pests responsible for damaging flowers and young shoots and for the sticky "drip" from some trees.

Hosing trees with plain or soapy water helps prevent and control problem pests such as aphids.

A neatly trimmed pink flowering dogwood *(Cornus florida)* in spring bloom with colorful azaleas and a purple Japanese maple.

Planting and Care of Flowering Trees

This chart presents in quick-reference form basic information about the planting requirements and follow-up care for each of the top-rated flowering trees discussed in this book. It is an easy guide to help you determine what conditions and care procedures the flowering trees you select for your garden will need to grow successfully. If a tree has varieties that are pest-resistant, it is listed as a pest-resistant plant.

PLANT NAME	Exposure			Water			Soil					Fertilizer			Pruning			Pest Resistant
	Sun	Partial Shade	Shade	Plenty	Regular	Drought Tolerant	Acid	Alkaline	Well-drained	Fertile	Infertile	Heavy	Regular	Light	Heading	Thinning	Season	
Acacia baileyana	■				■	■	■	■	■	■	■			■		■	late spring	yes
Aesculus x carnea	■				■	■	■	■	■	■			■	■		■	late spring	yes
Aesculus hippocastanum	■				■	■	■	■	■	■	■				■5		late spring	yes
Albizia julibrissin	■			■	■		■	■	■	■			■			■	late spring	no
Amelanchier sp.	■	■		■	■		■	■	■	■				■		■	late spring	yes
Bauhinia variegata	■			■	■		■		■	■			■			■	late spring	yes
Callistemon sp.	■			■	■	■	■	■	■	■	■		■	■	■5	■	early spring	yes
Cassia excelsa	■			■	■¹		■	■	■	■			■			■	after flowering	yes
Catalpa sp.	■				■		■	■	■	■	■		■	■		■	late winter	yes

¹ — Deep and infrequent
² — In desert areas
³ — Tolerates flooding
⁴ — Once established
⁵ — Takes shearing

PLANT NAME	Exposure			Water			Soil					Fertilizer			Pruning			Pest Resistant
	Sun	Partial Shade	Shade	Plenty	Regular	Drought Tolerant	Acid	Alkaline	Well-drained	Fertile	Infertile	Heavy	Regular	Light	Heading	Thinning	Season	
Cercis canadensis	■	■			■		■	■	■	■			■			■	late spring	yes
Cercis occidentalis	■	■			■	■	■	■	■	■	■			■		■	late spring	yes
Chionanthus virginicus	■	■		■	■		■		■	■		■	■			■	late winter	no
Citrus sp.	■	■		■	■		■	■	■	■		■	■		■[5]	■	early spring	no
Cornus florida	■	■		■			■		■	■			■			■	late winter	no
Cornus kousa	■	■		■	■		■		■	■			■			■	late winter	no
Crataegus sp.	■				■		■	■	■	■	■		■			■	late winter	no
Erythrina sp.	■			■	■				■	■			■			■	after flowering	yes
Eucalyptus sp.	■				■	■	■	■	■		■		■	■		■	spring	yes
Franklinia alatamaha	■	■		■	■		■		■	■		■	■			■	late winter	yes
Halesia carolina	■	■		■			■		■	■		■	■			■	after flowering	yes
Jacaranda mimosifolia	■				■		■	■	■	■			■			■	after flowering	yes
Koelreuteria bipinnata	■				■	■	■	■	■	■	■		■	■		■	late winter	yes
Koelreuteria paniculata	■				■	■	■	■	■	■	■		■	■		■	late winter	yes
Laburnum x watereri 'Vossii'	■	■[2]		■	■		■	■	■	■			■			■	late winter	yes
Lagerstroemia indica	■				■	■	■	■	■	■			■			■	late winter	no
Liriodendron tulipifera	■			■	■[4]		■		■	■			■			■	late winter	no
Magnolia grandiflora	■			■[3]	■		■	■	■	■			■	■		■	late summer	yes
Magnolia x soulangiana	■				■		■	■	■	■			■			■	late spring	yes
Magnolia stellata	■	■			■		■	■	■	■			■			■	after flowering	yes
Malus floribunda	■				■		■	■	■	■			■			■	late winter	yes
Malus 'Radiant'	■				■		■	■	■	■			■			■	late winter	yes
Malus 'Red Jade'	■				■		■	■	■	■			■			■	late winter	no

[1] — Deep and infrequent
[2] — In desert areas
[3] — Tolerates flooding
[4] — Once established
[5] — Takes shearing

PLANT NAME	Exposure			Water			Soil					Fertilizer			Pruning			Pest Resistant
	Sun	Partial Shade	Shade	Plenty	Regular	Drought Tolerant	Acid	Alkaline	Well-drained	Fertile	Infertile	Heavy	Regular	Light	Heading	Thinning	Season	
Malus 'Snowdrift'	■				■		■	■	■	■			■			■	late winter	no
Malus x zumi 'Calocarpa'	■				■		■	■	■	■			■			■	late winter	no
Melaleuca linariifolia	■				■	■	■	■	■	■	■		■	■		■	after flowering	yes
Melaleuca quinquenervia	■				■	■	■	■	■	■	■		■	■		■	after flowering	yes
Nerium oleander	■				■	■	■	■	■	■	■		■	■	■[5]	■	after flowering	yes
Oxydendrum arboreum	■			■			■		■	■			■			■	late winter	yes
Parkinsonia aculeata	■					■		■	■	■	■			■		■	late winter	yes
Prunus x blireiana	■				■		■	■	■	■			■			■	after flowering	no
Prunus caroliniana	■				■		■	■	■	■			■			■	after flowering	no
Prunus cerasifera 'Atropurpurea'	■				■		■	■	■	■			■			■	after flowering	no
Prunus x cistena	■				■		■	■	■	■			■			■	after flowering	no
Prunus serrulata	■				■		■	■	■	■			■			■	after flowering	no
Prunus subhirtella	■				■		■	■	■	■			■			■	after flowering	no
Pyrus calleryana 'Bradford'	■				■		■	■	■	■			■			■	after flowering	yes
Pyrus kawakamii	■	■			■		■	■	■	■			■			■	late spring	no
Robinia x ambigua 'Idahoensis'	■					■[4]	■	■	■	■	■		■	■		■	late winter	yes
Robinia pseudoacacia	■					■[4]	■	■	■	■	■		■		■[5]		late winter	yes
Sophora japonica	■				■	■	■	■	■	■			■	■		■	late winter	yes
Sorbus aucuparia	■				■		■	■	■	■			■			■	late winter	no
Stewartia pseudocamellia	■	■		■	■		■		■	■			■			■	late winter	yes
Styrax japonicus	■	■		■			■		■	■			■			■	late winter	yes
Wisteria floribunda	■				■		■	■	■	■	■		■	■		■	late winter	yes
Wisteria sinensis	■					■	■	■	■	■	■		■	■		■	late winter	yes

[1] — Deep and infrequent
[2] — In desert areas
[3] — Tolerates flooding
[4] — Once established
[5] — Takes shearing

Name Cross-Reference

A plant can have many common names but has only *one* proper botanical or scientific name. Some botanical names, because of their Latin origin, may be difficult to pronounce and remember at first, but become easier to use and more interesting as you become familiar with them. Common English plant names are often helpfully descriptive but they are too variable from person-to-person and place-to-place to be relied upon. The following list matches the most often used common names of flowering trees to their proper botanical names.

The parts of a botanical name that gardeners need to understand are the *genus, species,* and *cultivar* (or variety). The genus name signifies the general group to which the plant belongs, and together with the species name describes a particular plant. For instance, all cherries belong to the genus *Prunus,* and *Prunus serrulata* is the botanical name for Japanese flowering cherry.

The cultivar is the capitalized name between single quotation marks, for instance 'Rainbow' in *Cornus florida* 'Rainbow'. Cultivar stands for a cultivated variety. A cultivar is a plant that is propagated because of an outstanding feature that may or may not be perpetuated in nature. The cultivar may differ only slightly from the species or it may have significant differences, such as plant form, leaf color, or flower color. Botanical names that have an x between the genus and species, such as *Magnolia x soulangiana,* indicate the plant is a hybrid between two species, formed either naturally or by breeders.

Common Name	Botanical Name
Acacia, Bailey	*Acacia baileyana*
Bottlebrush, Lemon	*Callistemon citrinus*
Bottlebrush, Weeping	*Callistemon viminalis*
Buckeye	*Aesculus sp.*
Cajeput Tree	*Melaleuca quinquenervia*
Calamondin	*Citrus*
Catalpa, Common or Southern	*Catalpa bignonioides*
Catalpa, Northern or Western	*Catalpa speciosa*
Cherry, Higan	*Prunus subhirtella*
Cherry, Japanese Flowering	*Prunus serrulata*
Cherry, Weeping	*Prunus subhirtella*
Cherry Laurel, Carolina	*Prunus caroliniana*
Chinese Flame Tree	*Koelreuteria bipinnata*
Chinese Scholar Tree	*Sophora japonica*
Citrus	*Citrus sp.*
Cockspur Thorn	*Crataegus crus-galli*
Coral Tree	*Erythrina sp.*
Crab Apple, Flowering	*Malus sp.*
Crape Myrtle	*Lagerstroemia indica*
Crown of Gold Tree	*Cassia excelsa*
Dogwood, Flowering	*Cornus florida*
Dogwood, Japanese	*Cornus kousa*
Eucalyptus	*Eucalyptus sp.*
Flaxleaf Paperbark	*Melaleuca linariifolia*
Flowering Fruit	*Prunus sp.*
Franklin Tree	*Franklinia alatamaha*
Fringe Tree	*Chionanthus virginicus*
Golden-Chain Tree	*Laburnum x watereri* 'Vossii'
Golden-Rain Tree	*Koelreuteria paniculata*
Grapefruit	*Citrus*
Gum	*Eucalyptus sp.*
Hawthorn, English	*Crataegus laevigata*
Hawthorn, Lavelle	*Crataegus x lavallei*
Hawthorn, Washington	*Crataegus phaenopyrum*
Horse Chestnut, Common	*Aesculus hippocastanum*
Horse Chestnut, Red	*Aesculus x carnea*
Jacaranda	*Jacaranda mimosifolia*
Japanese Pagoda Tree	*Sophora japonica*
Jerusalem Thorn	*Parkinsonia aculeata*
Koelreuteria	*Koelreuteria sp.*
Kumquat	*Citrus*
Lemon	*Citrus*
Lime	*Citrus*
Locust, Black	*Robinia pseudoacacia*
Locust, Idaho	*Robinia x ambigua* 'Idahoensis'
Magnolia, Saucer	*Magnolia x soulangiana*
Magnolia, Southern	*Magnolia grandiflora*
Magnolia, Star	*Magnolia stellata*
Mandarin	*Citrus*
Melaleuca	*Melaleuca sp.*
Mimosa	*Albizia julibrissin*
Mountain Ash, European	*Sorbus aucuparia*
Oleander	*Nerium oleander*
Orange	*Citrus*
Orchid Tree, Purple	*Bauhinia variegata*
Paperbark, Flaxleaf	*Melaleuca linariifolia*
Pear, Bradford Callery	*Pyrus calleryana* 'Bradford'
Pear, Evergreen	*Pyrus kawakamii*
Plum, Blireiana	*Prunus x blireiana*
Plum, Purple-Leaf	*Prunus cerasifera* 'Atropurpurea'
Prunus	*Prunus sp.*
Purple-Leaf Sand Cherry	*Prunus x cistena*
Redbud, Eastern	*Cercis canadensis*
Redbud, Western	*Cercis occidentalis*
Serviceberry	*Amelanchier sp.*
Shadbush	*Amelanchier sp.*
Silk Tree	*Albizia julibrissin*
Silver-Bell	*Halesia carolina*
Silver-Dollar Tree	*Eucalyptus cinerea*
Snowbell, Japanese	*Styrax japonicus*
Sorrel Tree	*Oxydendrum arboreum*
Sourwood	*Oxydendrum arboreum*
Stewartia, Japanese	*Stewartia pseudocamellia*
Tangerine	*Citrus*
Tulip Tree	*Liriodendron tulipifera*
Wisteria, Chinese	*Wisteria sinensis*
Wisteria, Japanese	*Wisteria floribunda*
Yellow Poplar	*Liriodendron tulipifera*

Index

Main plant listings indicated by bold numbers.

A Acacia, Bailey, 9, 16, 19, **22**, 63
Acacia baileyana, 5, 9, 16, 19, **22**, 60, 63
Accent tree, 9
Aesculus, **22**, 63
 x *carnea*, 5, 17, **22**, 60, 63
 hippocastanum, 5, **22**, 60, 63
Albizia julibrissin, 5, 17, 19, **22**, **23**, 60, 63
Amelanchier sp., 5, 16, 17, 18, 19, **23**, **24**, 60, 63

B Balled-and-burlapped trees, 53
 planting, 54, 56
Bareroot trees, 53
 planting, 54
 pruning, 58, 59
Bark, ornamental, 17
Bauhinia purpurea, **24**
Bauhinia variegata, 5, 10, 16, **24**, 60, 63
Blossoms (see Flowers)
Bottlebrush, 17, 18, 19, **24**
 Lemon, 19, **24**, 53, 63
 Weeping, **24**, 63
Buckeye, **22**, 63

C Cajeput Tree, 19, **42**, 43, 63
Calamondin, **27**, 63
Callistemon, 5, 17, 18, 19, **24**, 60
 citrinus, 19, **24**, 53, 63
 viminalis, **24**, 63
Cassia excelsa, 5, 16, 17, **24**, 60, 63
Catalpa, 16, 17, 19, 21, **25**
 Common, **25**, 63
 Northern, **25**, **26**, 63
 Southern, **25**, 63
 Western, **25**, **26**, 63
Catalpa, 5, 16, 17, 19, 21, **25**, 60
 bignonioides, 14, **25**, 63
 speciosa, **25**, **26**, 63
Cercis, 12, 16, 17, 18, 19, **26**
 canadensis, 5, 17, **26**, 61, 63
 occidentalis, 5, 19, **26**, 61, 63
Cherry, Higan, **47**, 63
Cherry, Japanese Flowering, 45, **46**, **47**, 63
Cherry, Weeping, **47**, 63
Cherry Laurel, Carolina, **44**, **45**, 63
Chinese Flame Tree, **36**, 63
Chinese Scholar Tree, **49**, 63
Chionanthus virginicus, 5, 16, 17, 18, **26**, 27, 53, 61, 63
Citrus, 16, 18, **27**, 63
Citrus, 5, 9, 12, 16, 18, **27**, **28**, **29**, 61, 63
Climate
 hardiness map & zones, 4
 regional adaptation, 4; 5, 6, 7 (charts); 5 (map)
 microclimate, 4
Cockspur Thorn, 19, **32**, 63
Container-grown trees, 53
 planting, 56
Container plants, 11, 19
Coral Tree, 17, 19, 21, **32**, 63
 Cockspur, 17, **33**
 Kaffirboom, 3, 16, 19, **32**, 33
 Naked, **33**
 Natal, 32, **33**
Cornus, 2, 3, 16, 17, 18, 19, **29**, **30**
 florida, 5, 14, 16, 17, 19, **30**, 60, 61, 63
 kousa, 5, 14, **30**, **31**, 61, 63
Crab Apple
 Flowering, 3, 6, 16, 17, 18, 19, 20, 21, **40**, **41**, 42, 63
 Japanese Flowering, 16, 19, **41**
 Redbud Flowering, 16, **42**

Crape Myrtle, 9, 16, 17, 18, 19, **36**, **37**, 63
Crataegus, 5, 16, 17, 18, 19, **31**, **32**, 61
 crus-galli, 19, **32**, 63
 laevigata, 16, 17, 31, **32**, 63
 x *lavallei*, **32**, 63
 oxyacantha, **32**
 phaenopyrum, **32**, 63
Crown of Gold Tree, 16, 17, **24**, 63

D Deciduous, 11, 13, 14
Diseases, 23, 36, 41, 48, 58
Dogwood, 2, 3, 16, 17, 18, 19, **29**, **30**
 Flowering, 14, 16, 17, 19, **30**, 60, 63
 Chinese, **31**
 Japanese, 14, **30**, **31**, 63

E *Erythrina*, 17, 19, 21, **32**, 61, 63
 caffra, 3, 5, 16, 19, **32**, 33
 coralloides, 5, **33**
 crista-galli, 5, 17, **33**
 humeana, 5, 32, **33**
Espalier, 18
Eucalyptus, 16, 17, 18, 19, **33**, 63
Eucalyptus, 6, 16, 17, 18, 19, **33**, 61, 63
 cinerea, **34**, 63
 citriodora, 19, **34**
 ficifolia, 17, **34**
 gunnii, **34**
 polyanthemos, **34**
 viminalis, **34**
Evergreen, 11, 14, 15

F Fertilizing, 56, 57, 60, 61, 62
Flaxleaf Paperbark, **42**, 63
Flowering Fruit (see Prunus)
Flowers
 color lists, 16, 17
 color schemes, 12, 14
 fragrant, 18
 late color, 10
Franklinia alatamaha, 6, 16, 17, **34**, 61, 63
Franklin Tree, 16, 17, **34**, 63
Fringe Tree, 16, 17, 18, **26**, 27, 53, 63
Fruit
 colorful, 18
 for late color, 10
 ornamental & edible, 14

G Golden-Chain Tree, 16, 18, 19, **36**, 63
Golden-Rain Tree, 16, 17, 18, 19, **36**, 63
Grapefruit, 9, 28, 63
 'Marsh Seedless', **27**
 'Redblush', **27**, **28**
Gum, 63
 Cider, **34**
 Lemon-Scented, 19, **34**
 Manna, **34**
 Red, **34**
 Scarlet-Flowering, 17, **34**
 Silver-Dollar, **34**

H Habit, 11, 12
Halesia, 6
 carolina, 16, 18, 19, **34**, 35, 61, 63
 monticola, 19, **34**
Hawthorn, 16, 17, 18, 19, **31**, **32**
 English, 16, 17, 31, **32**, 63
 Lavelle, **32**, 63
 Washington, **32**, 63
Heading back, 58, 59
Horse Chestnut, 17, **22**, 63
 Red, 27, **22**, 63

I Insects, 26, 58, 59

J Jacaranda, 3, 16, 17, 19, **34**, **35**, 63
Jacaranda
 acutifolia, **34**, **35**
 mimosifolia, 3, 6, 16, 17, 19, **34**, **35**, 61, 63
 ovalifolia, **34**, **35**
Japanese Pagoda Tree, 16, 17, 18, 19, **49**, 63
Jerusalem Thorn, 16, 19, **44**, 63

K Koelreuteria, 16, 17, 18, 19, **36**, 63
Koelreuteria, 16, 17, 18, 19, **36**, 63
 bipinnata, 6, **36**, 61, 63
 paniculata, 6, 18, 19, **36**, 61, 63
Kumquat, 63
 'Nagami' Dwarf, **28**, 29

L *Laburnum* x *watereri* 'Vossi', 6, 16, 18, 19, **36**, 61, 63
Lagerstroemia indica, 6, 9, 16, 17, 18, 19, **36**, **37**, 61, 63
Landscaping
 landscape uses, 9-15
 selection aid, 14; 16-19 (lists)
 selecting a tree, 9
 site plan, 10, 11, 15
Lawn tree, 9
Lemon, 63
 'Eureka', **28**
 'Improved Meyer', **28**
Lime, 63
 'Bearss', **28**
 Persian, **28**
 Tahitian, **28**
Liriodendron tulipifera, 6, 17, **38**, 61, 63
Locust, **48**
 Black, 16, **48**, 49, 63
 Idaho, 16, 17, 18, 19, **48**, 63

M Magnolia, 16, **38**, **39**
 Saucer, 10, 16, 17, 18, 19, 39, **40**, 63
 Southern, 17, 18, 19, **39**, **40**, 63
 Star, 18, 19, 39, **40**, 63
Magnolia, 16, **38**, **39**
 grandiflora, 6, 17, 18, 19, **39**, **40**, 63
 x *soulangiana*, 6, 10, 16, 17, 18, 19, 39, **40**, 61, 63
 stellata, 18, 19, 39, **40**, 61, 63
Maintenance, 12, 60, 61, 62
Malus, 3, 6, 16, 18, 19, 20, 21, **40**, **41**, 42, 63
 floribunda, 6, 16, 19, **41**, 61
 'Radiant', 6, 17, 21, **42**, 61
 'Red Jade', 6, 16, 41, **42**, 61
 'Snowdrift', 6, 16, **42**, 62
 x *zumi* 'Calocarpa', 6, 16, **42**, 62
Mandarin, 63
 'Clementine', **29**
 'Dancy', **28**
 'Kara', **28**
 'Owari' Satsuma, **28**
Melaleuca, 16, 17, 19, **42**, 63
Melaleuca, 16, 17, 19, **42**, 63
 leucadendra, **42**
 linariifolia, 6, **42**, 62, 63
 quinquenervia, 6, 19, **42**, 43, 62, 63
Mimosa, 22, 23, 63
Mountain Ash
 European, 16, 17, 18, 19, **49**, **50**, 63
 Korean, **50**
Mulching, 56, 57

N *Nerium oleander*, 7, 10, 16, 17, 18, 19, 42, **43**, **44**, 62, 63

O Oleander, 10, 16, 17, 18, 19, 42, **43**, **44**, 63
Orange, 63
 'Chinotto' Sour, **28**, **29**
 'Valencia', **29**
 'Washington' Navel, 28, **29**
Orchid Tree, Purple, 10, 16, **24**, 63
Oxydendrum arboreum, 7, 16, 17, 18, **44**, 62, 63

P Paperbark, Flaxleaf, **42**, 63
Parkinsonia aculeata, 7, 16, 19, **44**, 62, 63
Pear, 16, 18, 19, **48**
 Bradford Callery, 12, 16, 17, **48**, 63
 Evergreen, 18, **48**, 63
pH (soil), 54
Planting, 54-56
Plum
 Blireiana, **44**, 63
 Purple-Leaf, **45**, **46**, 63
Privacy screen, 10
Pruning, 56, 58, 59, 60, 61, 62
Prunus, 3, 8, 9, 16, 17, 18, 19, **44**, 47, 63
Prunus, 3, 8, 9, 16, 17, 18, 19, **44**, 47, 63
 x *blireiana*, 7, **44**, 62, 63
 caroliniana, 7, **44**, **45**, 62, 63
 cerasifera 'Atropurpurea', 7, 44, **45**, **46**, 62, 63
 x *cistena*, 7, **46**, 62, 63
 serrulata, 7, 45, **46**, **47**, 62, 63
 subhirtella, 7, **47**, 62, 63
Purple-Leaf Sand Cherry, **46**, 63
Pyrus, 16, 17, 19, **48**
 calleryana 'Bradford', 7, 12, 16, 17, **48**, 62, 63
 kawakamii, 7, 18, **48**, 62, 63

R Redbud, 12, 16, 17, 18, 19, **26**
 Eastern, 17, **26**, 63
 Western, 19, **26**, 63
Robinia, **48**
 x *ambigua* 'Idahoensis', 7, 16, 17, 18, 19, **48**, 62, 63
 pseudoacacia, 7, 16, **48**, 49, 62, 63

S Serviceberry, 16, 17, 18, 19, **23**, **24**, 63
Shadbush, **23**, **24**, 63
Shade tree, 9
Shearing, 58
Silk Tree, 17, 19, **22**, **23**, 63
Silver-Bell, 16, 18, 19, **34**, 35, 63
Silver-Dollar Tree, **34**, 63
Site plan, 10, 11, 15
Snowbell, Japanese, 16, 17, 18, 19, **50**, 63
Soil, 54, 55, 60, 61, 62
Sophora japonica, 7, 16, 17, 18, 19, **49**, 62, 63
Sorbus
 alnifolia, **50**
 aucuparia, 7, 16, 17, 18, 19, **49**, **50**, 62, 63
Sorrel Tree, **44**, 63
Sourwood, 16, 17, 18, **44**, 63
Specimen tree, 9
Stewartia, Japanese, 16, 17, 18, **50**, 63
Stewartia pseudocamellia, 7, 16, 17, 18, **50**, 62, 63
Stopgap-filler, 10
Street tree, 9
Styrax japonicus, 7, 16, 17, 18, 19, **50**, 62, 63

T Tangerine, 63
 'Algerian', 12, **29**
Thinning, 58, 59
Tree selection, 12, 14, 16-19
Tulip Tree, 17, **38**, 63

W Watering, 54, 55, 56, 57, 60, 61, 62
Wisteria, 7, 16, 18, 21, **50**, **51**
 Chinese, **51**, 63
 Japanese, **51**, 63
Wisteria, 7, 16, 18, 21, **50**, **51**
 floribunda, 7, **51**, 62, 63
 sinensis, 7, **51**, 62, 63

Y Yellow Poplar, **38**, 63

Z Zones (see Climate)

C D E F